The Idea of
Continental Philosophy

A PHILOSOPHICAL CHRONICLE

D1610729

For Jennie

THE IDEA OF
CONTINENTAL PHILOSOPHY

A PHILOSOPHICAL CHRONICLE

Simon Glendinning

EDINBURGH UNIVERSITY PRESS

© Simon Glendinning, 2006

Edinburgh University Press Ltd
22 George Square, Edinburgh

Typeset in Sabon
by Servis Filmsetting Ltd, Manchester, and
printed and bound in Great Britain by
MPG Books Ltd, Bodmin, Cornwall

A CIP record for this book is available from the British Library

ISBN-10 0 7486 2470 8 (hardback)
ISBN-13 978 0 7486 2470 6
ISBN-10 0 7486 2471 6 (paperback)
ISBN-13 978 0 7486 2471 3

The right of Simon Glendinning
to be identified as author of this work
has been asserted in accordance with
the Copyright, Designs and Patents Act 1988.

Contents

1

Starting Points

An Initiation into Philosophy

I must have been about seventeen. From the hallway I could hear two of my older brothers talking very enthusiastically about things they were beginning to explore in their studies at university. They were talking about something called 'semiotics'. The door to the room was open as usual and I moved closer, cautiously approaching my spirited brothers inside. At the doorway I asked for an explanation, but whatever I was given just hung in the air and left me out of the charmed circle of my brothers' talk. I had no idea what they were on about and couldn't get into the conversation about French literary theory that they were then getting into.

About four years later something of all this must have been lurking still in the delight I felt on stumbling over John Locke's identification, on the very last page of my edition of the *Essay*, of '*Σημειωτική*' as one of the three most basic sorts of human inquiry.[1] I was delighted above all that I would now be able to recall for others (it has taken me a long time to get round to this) that a serious engagement with a 'doctrine of signs' under that title wasn't the special preserve of recent French thought.

That delightful discovery would come later in my time as a philosophy student, but my initial forays into this kind of talk at university left me more or less where I had been as a teenager: stationed firmly at the (I assumed open) doorway. In fact, the number of shiny words and closed conversations only grew, and their enigmatic obscurity became ever more exhausting. Third year and graduate students were now talking about 'postmodernism', 'poststructuralism', 'critical theory' and 'deconstruction', as well as 'semiotics'. And philosophical figures that remained largely invisible in an academic degree programme centred on the analytic tradition were also looming into some kind of hazy view: 'Hegel', 'Kierkegaard', 'Nietzsche', 'Marx', 'Heidegger', 'Adorno', 'Barthes', 'Derrida', 'Deleuze and Guatari', 'Irigaray' . . . I started to engage in a

1

serious effort to get my head round the basics of what was being called
'Continental philosophy'. I wanted to come to terms with this distinctive and alternative philosophical tradition.

And yet that effort only served to heighten my confusion. There
simply didn't seem to be a philosophical mast to pin one's colours to
round here – not *one* at any rate. Over the next six years or so I continued to read work by some of the big names of so-called Continental
philosophy. But despite many hours of often extremely profitable
reading I wasn't getting any closer to seeing how they might be grouped
together. It's not that these supposedly Continental philosophers
seemed to belong with the analytic philosophers I had come to know
in my university studies. Most clearly did not belong with them. But
they didn't seem to hang together either. The more I read the less sense
I could make of the idea that there was a distinctive tradition of philosophy in view here at all.

In 1996, shortly after getting my first full-time job as a philosophy
lecturer, I was invited by a commissioning editor from Edinburgh
University Press to put together an encyclopedia on Continental philosophy. At last, I thought, I had a real chance of getting the frustrating restlessness I had been experiencing hitherto over with. As Editor
I would have to write an Introduction in which I could (would have
to) finally sort out a view of my own, 'my view', on what Continental
philosophy is . . .

This book is an elaboration and development of that Editor's
Introduction.[2] And in this new text, as in the earlier one, I will defend
a view that ploughs a relentlessly sceptical furrow with respect to the
idea of a distinctive Continental tradition in modern philosophy. The
opening sentences of the earlier Introduction prepared the reader for
my doubts. I see now that they also generalise the initiation anxieties
that I have just related:

> Most people familiar with contemporary philosophy, particularly philoso-
> phy as it is taught at universities in the English-speaking world, will also be
> familiar with the category of 'Continental philosophy'. However, such famil-
> iarity typically extends no further than being able to say whether or not a
> given author is typically called a 'Continental philosopher'. Situations of this
> type normally reflect the shortcomings of a beginner or non-specialist, but
> in this case it seems to be more like a normal feature of the use of this label.
> Indeed, as I hope to show in this introduction, as a term of classification, the
> category of 'Continental philosophy' somewhat *lives* on being vague and
> free-floating.[3]

You can imagine that I was not entirely confident that my own account wouldn't just 'reflect the shortcomings of a beginner or non-specialist'. And so you can imagine too how relieved I was to find that, in fact, I was not alone in finding the idea of a distinctive Continental tradition so problematic. At the same time as I was writing my Introduction, one of the leading British authorities on phenomenology and deconstruction, Simon Critchley, was writing one too for the same sort of publication – and was (totally independently) coming to a (broadly) similar conclusion.[4] What gets included in Continental philosophy comprises, he suggested in his Introduction, 'a highly eclectic and disparate series of intellectual currents that could hardly be said to amount to a unified tradition',[5] and more strongly still he concluded that 'there is simply no category that would begin to cover the diversity of work produced by thinkers as methodologically and thematically opposed as Hegel and Kierkegaard, Freud and Buber, Heidegger and Adorno, or Lacan and Deleuze'.[6] Yes, yes.

Both Critchley and I identified a darker side to this odd story too. It also struck us both as deeply significant that the title of 'Continental philosophy' did not initially arise as a result of self-designation, but from a form of other-designation that Critchley called 'projection' and I called 'exclusion'. Here is Critchley with the basic point:

> Continental philosophy is an invention, or more accurately, a projection of the Anglo-American academy onto a Continental Europe that would not recognise the legitimacy of such an appellation – a little like asking for a Continental breakfast in Paris.[7]

The hunt for the inside track on Continental philosophy was over: there is no inside track to be found. Or at least that is what I had supposed and still suppose. As we shall see later in this book, Critchley thought otherwise and went on to affirm a positive, non-projective sense of a Continental tradition in philosophy. Since reading his 'Introduction' and later his book *Continental Philosophy: A Very Short Introduction* – a book which is, like this, an 'expanded' version of the earlier essay[8] – my ideas on the idea of Continental philosophy have developed with his in full view. However, although we are for long stretches fellow travellers, we are at crucial points quite sharply at odds. In particular, I remain convinced that his attempt to identify internal glue for a Continental tradition is doomed from the start. And not just doomed for him but for anyone: there is none.

It can sometimes seem hard to believe that this could be an even remotely plausible conclusion. My own upbringing in philosophy took place in a culture powerfully informed by the idea that the differences within in it should be comprehended in terms of the division between analytic and Continental philosophy. So the suggestion that the category of Continental philosophy is fundamentally ill-formed and problematic can seem hopelessly naive and scholastic. Yet I have gradually come to believe that, for the most part, recourse and reference to this division functions in a way that is more polemical and opportunistic than it is considered and well-founded. Even in contexts where no obvious judgement is being made about the quality of work being placed on either side, most appeals to the idea of a division or distinction between analytic and Continental philosophy seem to me at best troubling, and at worst simply awful.

This book aims to reconfigure our sense of the differences that inform our philosophical culture and tries to understand why those differences have been comprehended – and indeed *lived* – in terms which seem to me to be profoundly distorting and inadequate. In this chapter I will lay out three interpretive proposals which will guide my discussion throughout this book. I hope what I will say later on will reduce the dogmatic appearance of the proposals as they are introduced here. However, I want to be able to get going from what I consider to be the right starting points, and that requires getting ahead of the argument a little. Uncritical appeals to the schema 'analytic or Continental' betoken for me a failure to be alive to its (conceptual, existential, institutional) functioning and significance. I think we can do better than that and I want to try to do so from the start.

Interpreting Philosophy Today

Perhaps I shouldn't get so hung up about the problems with the division. It is not as if I don't know that there really are significant differences in the vicinity, differences which are often sufficient to ruin every effort to engage in positive discussion, let alone a critical dispute. I know things are bad, sometimes really bad. But – and here is my first interpretive proposal – in my view *appeals to the idea of division belong to what is so rotten here.* That is, in a situation where communication between different parts of our philosophical culture has all but broken down, the thinking about the breakdown that is an appeal to the idea of a division between analytic and Continental philosophy does not so much as capture the scene as it is *part of it*. It is itself a form of philosophical failure, a dimension of our inhabitation of the economy of our philosophical culture that is in so much of a hurry to say plainly 'what is what' that it is insensitive to the fundamentally questionable character of its own terms of trade.

So for some time now I have been trying to get to know what is going on here in a more measured way. And I keep concluding that a great many people who appeal to the division don't know what they are doing, don't know what they are talking about, don't know or don't want to know how the distinction is functioning in their discourse. It really is a fault in our culture.

Wanting to make things better the British philosophical logician Michael Dummett has said recently that it is only by going back to a point before the division occurred that we can hope to 're-establish communication', that 'it is no use now shouting across the gulf'.[9] I want to make things better too, and one of the reasons I think I can is that unlike many of my contemporaries I move around some of the supposedly gulf-separated texts in the stream of contemporary Western philosophy in ways which do not conform to this gulf-stricken image. I'm not saying, not pretending, that everything which finds a place in my life with philosophy is 'really the same' or that no one within me is shouting at anyone or failing to hear someone. Nor am I saying something of the kind that Dummett himself expressed when he found, to his surprise, that two seminal thinkers writing at the turn of the nineteenth century, Frege and Husserl, thinkers who he had supposed (because of the going terms of trade) should have been miles apart, were, in him, for him, not 'deeply opposed thinkers' but 'remarkably close in orientation despite some divergence of interests'.[10] I've also had that kind of experience, and it is an important one. But I don't want to ignore the other kind of experience, the experience of finding two writers who are supposed to be involved in the same subject speaking from radically different positions, positions which are not merely differences within (a given understanding of) philosophy but differences which attest to a conflict over what philosophy itself is or can be; differences over what can count as a philosophical remark or as a convincing appeal to people's attention; differences over what can be regarded as a responsible way of going on in philosophy. I have had that kind of experience too.

Nevertheless, I want my thinking about the situation here to be more cautious and more refined than one generally finds. As I see it, for the most part people seem happier to render inaccessible to themselves whatever they are (for some reason) interested in underestimating. And that, I think, is one of the main functions of the idea of an analytic/Continental split. It rationalises a willingness not to read, at least a willingness not to render oneself capable of reading well.

Of course one can't read everything, let alone read everything well. And I know too that philosophical writings that do not belong to the mainstream of analytic philosophy will typically be experienced as *distinctively difficult* to read by people whose studies are centred on that mainstream. However (and fully accepting that), there are two related interpretive responses to that distinctive difficulty that I want fundamentally to challenge:

1. the response that rationalises that difficulty by identifying such work as belonging to a distinctive Continental tradition of philosophy;
2. the response that sweeps the problem away by affirming that work in the Continental tradition does not typically represent the most responsible way of going on in philosophy.

The second, profoundly evaluative response is not something I could hope directly to challenge in this book. Not even an engagement with textual details could rebut that kind of charge. Since what counts as a responsible way of going on in philosophy is not something one can establish independently of having a high regard for a given way or ways of going on in philosophy, one would be looking to turn people round in their conception of the subject to an extent which no introduction is likely to achieve. However, I will want to confront the first interpretive response head on. And my hope is that this confrontation will not leave the second in such good shape. Again, I want to stress that the fact that I want to challenge the first of these responses should not be taken to suggest that I think that the kinds of works of philosophy that get identified in this way are really not so very different to works of analytic philosophy. As Dummett came to see some are not so very different, and that is important for everyone to realise since it shows that the differences are not always so sharp as is sometimes supposed. But that is not the basis of my objection to the response. The point is that even if I accept (as I do) that, in some more or less obvious and unexceptional sense, *none* of the writings identified as 'Continental' should be thought of as works from the tradition of analytic philosophy, I am under no obligation to accept the stronger response that they are works from a distinctively different Continental (or Modern European or whatever other name one wants to give it) tradition of philosophy. And here I want to enter a proposal – my second and most basic interpretive proposal – that provides a very strong reason for thinking that the current idea of division belongs to the scene of breakdown it aims to describe. The basic reason for thinking the current idea of division belongs to the rotten scene it aims to describe is that *there is no such thing as the tradition of Continental philosophy*.

That sounds very exciting. And in all the excitement it can lead to misunderstandings too. Since I want to call into question the very idea of Continental philosophy in this way it is very difficult for me to avoid giving the impression that something significant and perhaps rather obvious about the present philosophical culture is being overlooked or denied by my approach. An example of this effect will help illustrate some of the other things I have been touching on to this point. In a recent review of a book which collected interviews with a number of the younger generation of British philosophers, the philosopher of science Donald Gillies wrote of his surprise to see what he called 'a definite shift among new British philosophers away from the traditionally British analytic philosophy and towards Continental philosophy'.[11] Here we see the idea of the division within the contemporary philosophical culture between a traditionally British (or Anglophone) 'analytic' mode and a contrasting 'Continental' one appealed to in the way we might call *operational* rather than *thematic*: the idea of a difference is not the object of philosophical investigation so much as the matter of course resource for (meta)philosophising. Now, I am not certain that the same confidence in the distinction was really on show in all of the interviews in that book, but it is clear that Gillies did not think my thoughts on the matter had much going for them, and he wanted to see me as rather isolated in wanting to challenge the stereotypes in this area:

> One philosopher Simon Glendinning in his interview in chapter 12 puts forward the view that the difference between analytic and Continental philosophy is not an important one. As he says (p. 204): '. . . the analytic and Continental distinction . . . ultimately lacks any deep philosophical significance.' However, this view is not shared by any of the other philosophers who discuss the matter, and who assume there is a very significant difference between the two approaches to philosophy.

I am ruefully sure that I did not do myself many favours with that remark in the interview. At least that's how I feel now when I see it extracted from a context where I was trying positively to identify the philosophical issues which most deeply divide philosophers in our time, issues which I conceive as circulating around the relationship of philosophy to science and which I was sure then as now cannot be held within the frame of the analytic/Continental difference. In any case, the burden of my argument was not at all to suggest that the analytic/Continental difference 'is not an important one' as Gillies puts it for me (do the words he cites really support that strong construal?), but rather to identify or specify the kind of importance, the kind of philosophical significance, it has. Indeed, in my defence I might note that I explicitly stressed that my approach 'does *not* mean that the account of the growth of the distinction and division, the developing idea of a wide gulf, has no philosophical significance'.[12] The division belongs *centrally* to the understanding of Western philosophy as it goes on today, and one cannot move without bumping into it – as 'the other philosophers who discuss the matter' in the interviews also significantly show. Since I think that the very idea of a distinctive Continental tradition – a way of going on in philosophy with its own distinctive style, method or problematic field – is deeply questionable I can hardly accept that the analytic/Continental distinction is, as such, of 'deep philosophical significance'. That it touches all of us (all the time and sometimes deeply), however, is simply beyond question, and I have never suggested otherwise.

Still, I have clearly given the impression that I wanted to ignore something important about the present situation. And it is worth reminding ourselves of the force of a distinction which still dominates (and for some has really messed up) the lives of philosophers in our time. While insisting that the differences 'between so-called Continental and Anglo-Saxon philosophies' *cannot* be understood in terms of intraphilosophical 'questions of style, method or even problematic field', Jacques Derrida, writing back in 1978, summarised well a situation in which,

> [differences] are sometimes so serious that the minimal conditions for communication and co-operation are lacking. The minimal contract of a common code is no longer ensured, and when I speak of a code I do not mean only the strictly linguistic element of these rules of exchange. Within a single linguistic area, for example, the Anglophone world of Britain and America, the same interference or opacity can prevent philosophical communication and even make one doubt the unity of *the* philosophical, of the concept or project behind the word *philosophy*, which then constantly risks being but a homonymic lure.[13]

For Derrida – and I think he is right about this – the breakdown 'between *so-called* [note that careful attention to a questionable name] Continental and Anglo-Saxon philosophies' can 'sometimes [note that equally scrupulous attention to the variability of the difficulty]' suffice to make the idea of philosophy itself, the idea of a distinctive form of inquiry, a specific mode of questioning among others, seem 'precarious and enigmatic'.[14] We are quite close (and in view of the attention to details, also quite far) with this worry to the British moral philosopher R. M. Hare's view, stated some twenty years earlier, and to which I will return later in this book, that philosophy as it stands in our time is not (or is no longer) one: there are, he boldly claimed in 1960, 'two different ways' in which philosophy is now studied, ways concerning which 'one might be forgiven for thinking . . . are really two quite different subjects'.[15] As Dummett put it more recently 'we have reached a point at which it is *as if* we're working in different subjects'.[16]

If only there really were now two subjects, if only it were now such that it was more than only '*as if*' it were so, if only the title really was now nothing but 'a homonymic lure' masking the fact that the contemporary inheritance of the subject that used to be called philosophy had bifurcated into two different subjects . . . If only all that were true then everything would be so much simpler. The differences would be tractable, traceable to identifiable differences of style, method or problematic field of the two subjects. But it is not. And that non-simplicity, for me, is quite enough to demand of us something better, something more refined than a machine-like reiteration of the assumption that what is at issue 'is a very significant difference between the two approaches to philosophy'. That the situation is one in which the philosophical culture is at times deeply divided, divided in ways which are 'sometimes so serious' as to make communication nearly impossible, is, as I say, beyond question. But precisely because of the 'precarious and enigmatic' condition of philosophy today, a serious engagement with the nature and significance of that all too secure and clear idea of division is, it seems to me, a timely one. In any case that is what I am going to attempt in this book.

A measure of the distinction's power and cultural reach today was brought home to me recently when I was getting ready to leave a party. I was just putting my jacket on to go home when someone said to me 'Ah, now you look the complete *Continental* philosopher'.[17] The pertinence of the friendly remark (and the reason it took putting a black leather jacket on to look the part) would not be lost on anyone who is at all familiar with contemporary images of Continental intellectuals. The distinction between that (supposedly) rather exotic breed of *engagé* thinkers and their (supposedly) less glamorous and sedentary Anglo-Saxon or Anglo-American or Anglophone analytic version is very precisely recorded by Simon Critchley, someone who (I think) knows very well what one should wear when:

> One is used to thinking of the distinction between the analytic and Continental traditions [in terms] where analytic philosophy is conservative and stuffy in a sort of senior common room, leather arm-patch sort of way, and Continental philosophy is its funky streetwise, leather-jacketed obverse.[18]

The idea of being (or at least appearing to be) something of a radical, a roguish outsider to the dominant establishment and the mainstream, is often considered central to the ethos of those who engage in Continental philosophy today, and it may even be what draws some people towards it. Those who these days take the title for themselves – wherever they live or work – commonly see what they do as an attempt to revitalise the discipline, offering as one subscriber in America puts it, 'a way out of the doldrums that philosophy has accomplished for itself in the past several decades'.[19] So it can all seem so very vital, so very different from the arid-seeming terrain of the analytic mainstream. (That's not totally wrong.)

Of course, things look rather different from the terrain of the analytic mainstream. Doldrums? What doldrums? 'You may find our arguments dry, but do you really think the barely readable, esoteric, *ex cathedra* words of your Continental masters are going to revitalise anything . . .' (That's not totally wrong either.)

And so it goes on. But with this difference of perception – a difference I can readily acknowledge myself – something becomes visible that is of enormous significance to an understanding of the idea of an analytic/Continental division in general: namely, that it belongs to a bifurcation in what I want to call *reception-responses*. More specifically, what is at issue with the idea of Continental philosophy is the reception 'over here' of work that is going on 'over there'.

In this context 'over here' now designates something like 'from the English-speaking world'. However, for reasons that are far from negligible, this English-language reception context is, in fact, originally, a British one. It is not only that the spatial designators (over here/over there) work better from Britain (we really can point from here, it is that close), the very title 'Continental' clearly signals a British source. The

English word 'continent' (deriving from Latin sources from which we also get the word 'container') had, by the middle of the seventeenth century, already taken on its current geographical sense of 'a vast land-mass not broken by seas', but around this time, when preceded by a definite article (and often with a capitalised initial), it was also beginning to be used as the name for 'the mainland of Europe, as distinguished from the British Isles'. The idea of the Continent is in itself a designation from over here of a place which is, essentially, over there. There is a reference to an elsewhere inscribed in the name, and this is something that the idea of Continental philosophy imports into itself from its British origins. The British title may now have travelled the world, and was unquestioningly taken up by most of the American philosophical academy some forty years ago now,[20] but there are trailing clouds of British history which are not sloughed off in this passage, and the idea of Continental philosophy is never radically free of its taint of being that form of (broadly speaking) Western philosophy that is *not what we do round here* – most of us anyway, those who have managed not to succumb to what a Cambridge don recently called the 'common taste for mystification' or 'inflated trivialities' of many of his colleagues in the humanities.[21]

Now, saying it is not what we do round here may be regarded 'purely descriptively', but there is no doubt that for the majority of philosophers in the English-speaking world during the twentieth century the idea of Continental philosophy has had a profoundly *evaluative* accent, representing quite precisely what is beyond the pale philosophically speaking – the Cambridge don's dig is a cat coming out of the bag. It is not only *What we do not do*, but *What ought not be done* if one wants to think seriously within the central channels of the Western philosophical tradition. On this view, the idea of Continental philosophy is the idea of a kind of bastard offshoot of that tradition, an offshoot which, although in a very broad sense part of the history of the subject, is not part of the central strand. Specifically, it is an offshoot that is marked by a kind of failure of inheritance, an abandonment of the standards which should characterise properly philosophical inquiry. Thus authors engaged in what, at least since the time of J. S. Mill, British philosophy has been calling 'the Continental philosophy' are regarded as doing work which is not only of a supposedly distinctive kind but also, it must be said, of a decidedly *inferior* quality.[22]

During the second half of the twentieth century this view came to dominate philosophical institutions right across the English-speaking

11

world. No English-speaking philosopher educated since the late 1950s could fail to appreciate that 'Continental philosophy' is regarded as the harbinger of all that is 'arbitrary, pretentious and soul-destroying' in contemporary thought, wherever it is written.[23]

So the idea of Continental philosophy, and the idea of participating in a distinctive Continental tradition, does not actually emerge from where one might have thought it should have emerged from. In fact, it is difficult even to articulate the idea in a language other than English. (It is notable that the Collins-Robert dictionary (1992) details the capitalised use of 'Continental' in the English/French section but not in the French/English section.) In this respect, as we have seen Critchley point out already, the use of the title 'Continental philosophy' can be compared to that of a 'Continental breakfast'. No one who lives on mainland Europe would have thought of giving their morning meal that name, but now there is not only a kind of breakfast called a 'Continental breakfast', it is possible to eat one anywhere. In fact, it is now a truly intercontinental phenomenon. One can ever order it, to some bemusement of the locals, on the Continent.

Some parallel points can be made about Continental philosophy. It is not simply that, as it is understood today, it can now be 'done' elsewhere or anywhere, but the generic sense it now has is of a style or species of philosophy which *can* be done anywhere. It can be done in America or Australia too, or, again, on the Continent.

Of course, this understanding assumes that there really *is* something which has an identity sufficiently robust to be spotted, repeated and here or there indulged in. While I am happy to concede that this is now the case with a Continental breakfast, I am far less confident that the same can be said for Continental philosophy. In the chapters that follow I will argue that the very idea of a fruitfully distinguishable philosophical tradition of Continental philosophy is, first and foremost, part of the mythological history of (the movement that came to call itself) analytic philosophy. That is, and this is my third interpretive proposal, *the very idea of such a tradition is best thought of as an item that has its original home in the conceptual armoury of analytic philosophy.* In this respect, 'Continental philosophy' is less the name for an other kind of philosophy than analytic philosophy, but a term that functions *within* analytic philosophy as the name of its own other, that part of its lexicon which represents what is '*not part*' of it. In what follows I will often say that Continental philosophy is, for this reason, 'the Other' of analytic philosophy. The point of this capitalisation is visually to mark a difference (which I think is actual) between modes of philosophy that are not part of the mainstream of contemporary analytic philosophy (they are genuinely other to analytic philosophy) and analytic philosophy's own conception of those modes as comprising a distinctive and significantly different approach to philosophy (the Other of analytic philosophy).

As we shall see in later chapters, analytic philosophy itself *suffers* from this understanding. However, as I have already indicated, there is a complication to this point brought about by the fact that, in recent years, many people have appropriated the title positively to define what they do themselves. I will delve into that recent history later, and when I do I will show that the appropriation of this title for a vital 'new wave'[24] in philosophy is, as many of the advocates of the idea know full well, essentially separable from the (I think) totally implausible suggestion that their work relates to a distinctive Continental tradition of philosophy.

So we have three interpretive proposals:

1. In a situation where communication has all but broken down between self-styled analytic philosophers and other voices in the contemporary philosophical culture, the thinking about the breakdown that is an appeal to the idea of a division between analytic and Continental philosophy does not so much as capture the rotten scene as it is part of it.
2. There is no such thing as the tradition of Continental philosophy
3. The idea of a distinctive Continental tradition is best thought of as an item in the conceptual armoury of analytic philosophy; it is the idea of its own Other.

To conclude this chapter I want briefly to clarify the second and perhaps most radical of these proposals.

A Working Distinction: Works of and Works in

My approach to the topic of this book is iconoclastic, but I hope that it will not be regarded as inaccurate or unrealistic, nor indeed unsympathetic to those in the English-speaking world (or anywhere else for that matter) who now (or now and then) take the title of Continental philosophy for what they do, myself included. In order to clarify the historical and institutional situation as I see it I am going to make use of a distinction between, on the one hand, writings as they are

	Frege	Russell	Vienna Circle	Quine	Oxford	TLP	PI
Linguistic turn	✗	✗	✓	✓	✓	✓	✓
Rejection of metaphysics	✗	✗	✓	✗	(✓)	(✓)	✓
Philosophy ≠ science	(✗)	✗	(✓)	✗	✓	✓	✓
Reductive analysis	(✗)	✓	✓	(✓)	✗	✓	✗
Formal logic	✓	✓	✓	✓	(✗)	✓	✗
Science oriented	✓	✓	✓	✓	✗	✗	✗
Argument	✓	✓	(✓)	(✓)	✓	(✗)	(✓)
Clarity	✓	✓	✓	(✓)	✓	✗	(✗)

Figure 1.1 *Analytic philosophy at a glance.*

gathered under a certain title ('works *of* X') and, on the other hand, writings as they are committed to a certain outlook or adhere to a certain methodological conception ('works *in* X').[25] Now, one might expect that the sets of works identified by these specifications to be co-extensional. So while the relations between different texts may be complex and marked more by Wittgensteinian family resemblances rather than by ubiquitous common features, it would seem unproblematic to affirm, for example, that 'the primary works *of* logical positivism' precisely comprise those texts that are 'the primary works *in* logical positivism'. Can the same be said of analytic philosophy? Although the family resemblances are less determinate in this case, in a rough and ready way I think it can. Hanjo Glock provides a conceptual schema which seems to me to capture things very nicely in this area (see Figure 1.1).[26]

If you tick the majority of the boxes you are an analytic philosopher, if you do not you are not. Glock's table gives a few illustrative examples from the movement of analytic philosophy, but it is instructive to try it out on any of those who do *not* normally count as analytical philosophers as well. And it seems to me that people who do not normally count don't count here either.[27] Doubtless this result would provide an opening for the idea that these authors belong to a distinctively different tradition in contemporary philosophy. However, the fact that one can produce a set in this way (a set formed by virtue of its members sharing the property of 'not being an analytic philosopher') does not mean that one has unearthed a tradition: there are an indefinite number of ways of not being something. As I hope to show, coming to appreciate (if not exactly to admire) why certain texts have been brought together as the Continental collection helps one clearly to see why what one can in this way call the primary works *of* Continental philosophy do not comprise the primary works *in* it.

In order to account for the more recent idea that Continental philosophy is a distinctive and vital 'new wave' on the contemporary philosophical scene I will, in due course, need to complicate matters somewhat and add the further category of 'works *on* works *of* Continental philosophy'. To complicate matters further still these works tend to go by the name of 'studies *in* Continental philosophy'. However, my claim will be that even the most exemplary and influential of such writings remain historically and methodologically *secondary* to the major works *of* Continental philosophy that they engage with, and so do not, in that sense, comprise '*primary* texts *in* Continental philosophy' either. My second interpretive proposal can be helpfully reformulated like this: *there are no primary texts* in *Continental philosophy*.

Even this refinement of my second and most blunt proposal may seem too blunt. After all, the authors and texts which are typically grouped together under this title, the various 'currents of thought'[28] or 'philosophical practices'[29] that are brought together under the single banner, *are* more or less (sometimes more, sometimes less) closely related to each other. For this reason it might be thought that my rejection of the very idea of a distinctive tradition in this case must presuppose an unhelpful and far too demanding understanding of what does and what does not constitute a *tradition* in the first place. For example, am I saying that a set of texts can only belong to a philosophical tradition if they all or nearly all share certain basic principles or assumptions? Aren't traditions just a bit more rough-and-ready, a bit more unprincipled than that?

In fact, as I hope should already be evident, I am completely convinced that traditions are *not* formal unities, *not* fully rational structures. Hence, I do not suppose that the fact that there are clear objections to the idea that there is a recognisable or determinate methodological kernel or characteristic outlook shared by the primary texts of Continental philosophy automatically discredits the idea that there is good reason to think that what is at issue here may, indeed, be a distinctive tradition in it. No, what discredits that idea is something else, something that most experts working in the field know full well: namely, the fact that what gets grouped together as the primary works of Continental philosophy 'is a highly eclectic and disparate series of intellectual currents that could hardly be said to amount to a unified tradition'[30] or, again, and more pointedly that 'there is simply no category that would begin to cover the diversity of work produced by thinkers as methodologically and thematically opposed as Hegel and Kierkegaard, Freud and Buber, Heidegger and Adorno, or Lacan and Deleuze'.[31] That is all, but if it is right it should be quite enough to ruin the suggestion of a distinctive tradition.

So while the thinkers and movements that are usually included under the banner do comprise, as one commentator has put it, 'a variety of more or less closely related currents of thought',[32] this does not, in my view, justify talk of a distinctive tradition. Indeed, so weak is the internal bonding in this group that analytic philosophers are often 'more or less closely related' (sometimes more, sometimes less) to them too. Thus, in my view, what these interrelations really point towards is ultimately the profound 'enigma' of philosophy itself as a subject touched on earlier. I mean, what holds them *all* together – analytic and non-analytic, and all among each other – is about as far from being a simple matter as one can get. The question 'What is philosophy?' is itself a question in the subject that goes by the name 'philosophy'. And there is, I think, no way out of that interpretive and contested circle.

The Wittgensteinian image of family resemblances helps us to understand how a conceptual unity can tolerate a wide diversity of cases. However, it can also be invoked to support a certain way of going on with the idea of the division of the contemporary culture that I find just as misleading and unhelpful as more cut and dry views. In ecumenical spirit someone might say 'Of course there is no rigid division, no unbridgeable chasm between analytic and Continental philosophy. There is a spectrum of cases, and they shade over in the middle'. What is right in that spectrum image is the idea that the different movements or currents in the stream of Western philosophy typically shade across each other. But the mistake is to think of that stream as amenable to a cross-section that divides it roughly into two: that there is one (transverse) line running across the river with, as it were, Logic at one bank and Poetry at the other, and a fuzzy overlapping bit in the middle. The banal truth is that there are various currents in the contemporary philosophical culture and they sweep and seep into each other at various points and in various ways, and sometimes they are not close at all.[33] There is no future in erasing such differences and trying to make everyone seem the same, neither when we are looking at differences between thinkers who are in the analytic mainstream and thinkers who are not, nor when we are looking at differences between the motley of thinkers who are not. In the chapters that follow I will try to show that existing attempts to justify the idea that the primary works of Continental philosophy comprise something like a philosophical tradition that stands in a more or less clear contrast to the analytic tradition are (in various ways) inadequate. More ambitiously, I will try to show too that these inadequacies could not be overcome by a more powerful or more nuanced account. I will also try to indicate where this leaves those working and thinking within the current philosophical culture, steeped as it still is in the idea of a distinctive 'Continental mode' of pursuing philosophy.

Notes

1. John Locke, *An Essay Concerning Human Understanding*, ed. A. D. Woozley, Glasgow: Collins, 1964, p. 443. The most natural modern-English translation of '*Σημειωτική*' would be, of course, precisely, 'Semiotics'.
2. Simon Glendinning, 'Introduction', *Encyclopedia of Continental Philosophy*, ed. S. Glendinning, Edinburgh: EUP, 1999. A more recent version of that Introduction is published in *Fundamentals of Philosophy*, ed. J. Shand, London: Routledge, 2003.
3. Simon Glendinning, 'Introduction', p. 3.
4. Simon Critchley, 'Introduction', in *A Companion to Continental Philosophy*, eds S. Critchley and W. Schroeder, Oxford: Blackwell, 1998.
5. Simon Critchley, 'Introduction', p. 5.
6. Simon Critchley, 'Introduction', p. 6.
7. Simon Critchley, 'Introduction', p. 5.
8. Simon Critchley, *Very Short Introduction to Continental Philosophy*, Oxford: OUP, 2001, p. 137.
9. Michael Dummett, cited in Critchley, *Very Short Introduction to Continental Philosophy*, p. 15.
10. Michael Dummett cited in Critchley, *Very Short Introduction to Continental Philosophy*, p. 15.
11. David Gillies's review of *New British Philosophy: The Interviews*, eds J. Baggini and J. Strangroom, London: Routledge, 2002, 'Some Reflections on New British Philosophy' is posted at http://www.kcl.ac.uk/kis/schools/hums/*philosophy/frames/Staff/Gillies/newbritishphilosophy.html*. The Appendix to this book will offer considerable support for Gillies perception of a shift in the cultural formation of philosophy in Britain in recent years. Everything which precedes the Appendix will, however, call into question his way of articulating that shift.
12. Simon Glendinning, *New British Philosophy: The Interviews*, p. 205.
13. Jacques Derrida, *Who's Afraid of Philosophy*, Stanford, CA: Stanford University Press, 2002, p. 104.
14. Jacques Derrida, *Who's Afraid of Philosophy*, p. 104.
15. R. M. Hare 'A School for Philosophers', *Ratio*, vol. 2, no. 2, 1960, p. 107.

16. Michael Dummett, cited in Critchley, *Very Short Introduction to Continental Philosophy*, p. 15. Emphasis mine.
17. Kevin O'Sullivan (personal communication).
18. Simon Critchley, *Very Short Introduction to Continental Philosophy*, p. 45.
19. Hugh Silverman, *Philosophy and Non-Philosophy since Merleau-Ponty*, ed. H. J. Silverman, London: Routledge, 1988, p. 2.
20. John McCumber has suggested that the term crossed the big pond (another British expression which indicates a (different) kind of proximity of an 'over there') 'in the mid 1960's' (John, McCumber, *Time in the Ditch*, Evanston, IL: Northwestern University Press, 2001, p. 50).
21. Nicholas Denyer, 'The Charms of Jacques Derrida', *Cambridge Review*, vol. 113, no. 2318, October 1992, p. 104.
22. Simon Critchley has identified two essays by Mill from the 1830s and 1840s which may be the first writings in print to make use of the terms 'Continental philosophers' and 'the Continental philosophy' (Simon Critchley, *Very Short Introduction to Continental Philosophy* , p. 42). It should be remembered, however, that Mill himself conceived his own work as in crucial ways trying to *overcome* an antagonism between what he called 'English' and 'Continental' thought about politics – between a mode of political thought based fundamentally on a theory of human *nature* (the outlook of his father(s) with its roots in Cicero's attempt to derive a – political – theory of human nature from Plato) and one based on a view of human *history* (an outlook with its roots in Polybius' attempt to derive a – political – theory of human history from Plato). Mill retained a priority of the psychological over the historical but his own position is strikingly 'mixed'. This series of footnotes to Plato is brilliantly outlined in Robert Cumming's study of the development of liberal thought *Human Nature and History* (2 vols, Chicago: Chicago University Press, 1969). We might note for the record that Cumming regards the result of Mill's reconciliation as the effective transformation of political theory into what Mill calls 'mental history', i.e. into the history of ideas. Cumming calls this turn to a genre that is 'slacker than philosophy' (Vol. 2, p. 432) 'a final and fatal weakening' of traditional political philosophy (Vol. 2, p. 426).
23. John Passmore, *A Hundred Years of Philosophy*, London: Penguin, 1957, p. 467.
24. Hugh Silverman, *Philosophy and Non-Philosophy since Merleau-Ponty*, p. 2.
25. I am indebted to conversations with Peter Osborne for showing me the significance of this distinction, and will cite his own formulation of it in the final chapter. The main argument of this book develops and I hope systematically accounts for Osborne's hunch that in the case of Continental philosophy the two dimensions come apart. I will not always advert to the distinction with italics but the reader should be aware that I always try to keep the distinction in view.
26. H.-J. Glock, 'Was Wittgenstein an Analytic Philosopher?', *Metaphilosophy*, vol. 35, no. 4, 2004, p. 438. A crucial element that remains

totally unrepresented in this schema is something that Simon Critchley emphasises, perhaps equally one-sidedly, as 'what matters' with respect to whether on is 'in' or 'out' of a tradition: namely, the question of 'which tradition the philosopher feels part of' (Simon Critchley, 'Introduction', p. 9). So while I think that Glock's table will give a fairly reliable prediction of who is 'in' and who is 'out' of the analytic movement that does not mean that it can be relied upon (at all really) to explain what makes people *feel* 'in', still less whether those who are 'out' belong together or not. It is not, in that sense, an analysis of a widely shared idea of analytic philosophy. As Glock is aware, most people who provide 'doctrinal definitions' of analytic philosophy define it in terms of what they think it *ought* to be (with definitions which express their own commitments, and so express why they themselves feel part of the movement), and so are, as predictors, always 'too narrow' (H.-J. Glock, 'Was Wittgenstein an Analytic Philosopher?', p. 429).

27. Glock's parentheses indicate either that he regards the verdict as 'contestable' or that the feature is 'partly present or partly absent'. A distinctive feature of this table is that it makes perspicuous the central place of the Vienna Circle in the self-understanding of the analytic movement, something Glock thinks is historically undeniable and which many more recent analytic philosophers would either resist or want to forget. However, in that regard one should not infer that because Vienna Circle thinkers tick all the analytic boxes they belong together in a philosophical school with determinate frontiers. If one were to make a table that detailed the family traits of the Vienna Circle one would want to add additional parameters. In a personal communication, Glock noted that, in particular, one would need to include a parameter that would mark 'the split between those who accepted a Wittgensteinian *distinction* between philosophy and science (Schlick, Carnap, Waismann) and those who rejected it (Neurath, Hahn)'. One should also bear in mind that (as Glock himself acknowledges) the case for an individual philosopher's placement on this or any other such 'at a glance' table is not itself typically judgeable at a glance and that different kinds of philosophy might call into question the criteria of (for example) clarity and argument that most analytic philosophers would cleave to in making such judgements. For a rough count of the varieties of clarity one might seek in philosophy – and the common-sense criteria for stylistic clarity that Glock is (not unproblematically) relying on here – see H.-J. Glock, ' "Clarity" is not Enough', in *Wittgenstein and the Future of Philosophy: Proceedings of the 24th International Wittgenstein Symposium*, eds R. Haller and K. Puhl, Vienna: Hölder-Pichler-Tempsky, 2002, pp. 81–98.

28. David West, *An Introduction to Continental Philosophy*, Oxford: Polity, 1996, p. 1.

29. Hugh Silverman, *Philosophy and Non-Philosophy since Merleau-Ponty*, p. 1

30. Simon Critchley, 'Introduction', p. 5.

31. Simon Critchley, 'Introduction', p. 6.

32. David West, *An Introduction to Continental Philosophy*, p. 1.

33. In the final chapter I will employ the spectrum image myself to represent various possible relations that philosophers with a serious working interest in non-analytic kinds of philosophy might have to the primary texts of analytic philosophy. But by that stage the image will not be used to mark distinctions between philosophers who are more or less 'Continental' (in view of their distance from an analytic mainstream), but simply to map an array of reading and research interests that focus *more* or *less* exclusively on non-analytic figures and resources.

2

A Meeting of (Some) Minds: Phenomenology at Large

A Wide-Angled View

In the last chapter I proposed that the thinking about the breakdowns in communication within the contemporary philosophical culture that appeals to the idea of a division between the traditions of analytic and Continental philosophy is part of and does not stand apart from the rotten scene it intends to capture. The plausibility of this proposal would be massively increased if I could demonstrate the independent plausibility of a further proposal: namely, that the very idea of a distinctive Continental tradition in philosophy is confused and distorting. It is a basic aim of this book to substantiate that. In doing so I do not intend to deny that the philosophical movements that are collectively grouped together under the 'Continental' title comprise 'a variety of more or less closely related currents of thought'.[1] However, what I do reject is the idea that what we have in view here can be satisfactorily understood as a philosophical tradition or traditions standing in a crucial contrast to the analytic tradition. Yes, the currents of thought at issue *are* more or less closely related, but that is because what is in view here is a great swathe of the enigmatic diversity that currently comprises the contested subject that is called 'philosophy', not because it comprises a special subset of that subject that distinctively belongs together in contrast to the analytic tradition. In the last chapter I used a text by Donald Gillies to illustrate an operational rather than thematic interest in the idea of a division of traditions. In this chapter I want to turn things round and reflect on how things can look if we take a view of the philosophical culture in which the prism of the analytic/Continental idea is the object of investigation rather than the matter of course resource for (meta)philosophising. I will call this the wide-angled view. Taking this view will not establish the problematic character of the idea of Continental philosophy. But it will show us how things can look when one tries to forgo it. And that is a start.

When we look at the turbulent waters of contemporary thought from this wide-angled view one of the first things to become newly salient is that despite having made little impact on the wider intellectual culture (and even very little impact on other academic disciplines) the analytic movement clearly belongs among the major intellectual movements that most profoundly characterise the cultural world of Europe and the West today. As a movement, it is true, it is marked by its own insistence on marking itself out – in crayon as it were – by asserting its difference from the direction taken by much of the rest of the intellectual world of the West, and in particular by its insistence on its difference from what it regards as a supposedly distinctive 'Continental' trajectory. But, as we shall see in some detail later in this book, the fact is that what most analytic philosophers want to engage with today, the issues and questions which they find it compelling to attend to, belong to precisely the same problematic field (what Robert Pippin calls 'the problem of modernity') as do other movements in Western philosophy.

Of course, the crayon work is far from negligible. As Hilary Putnam has noted, when he was a student one became an analytic philosopher by learning 'what *not* to like and what not to consider philosophy'.[2] It has been said that nations find their unity through their dislike of their neighbours and a misunderstanding of their own past. In this respect analytic philosophy might be regarded as the photographic negative of a nation: as we shall see in later chapters of this book, it has found a unity through a dislike of what went before it, and a misunderstanding of its neighbours.

This does not make it a movement with an especially fragile identity. What has emerged here is a powerful and resilient creature that, as we saw in the last chapter, can be fairly well characterised quite independently of its relation to what it calls 'Continental philosophy'. However, its self-discrimination within the wider intellectual world is not typically drawn independently of that relation, and I hope to show that the robust sense that it maintains concerning its own relative philosophical health is also a kind of philosophical flaw, something it suffers from. That is to come, however. For the moment let's stay with the wide-angled view of the contemporary philosophical culture.

The wide angle does not obliterate every difference. Keeping with the river metaphor, if one's view aims to take in the deep and turbulent stream of Western philosophical thought one can still follow various (sometimes more, sometimes less) discernable currents and flows within it. One of the things a historian of philosophy today cannot ignore is that some of the movements within the philosophical stream are sufficiently well differentiated from other parts that one can discern a way of going on in philosophy that can be followed without much attention needing to be given to affiliations with or to the texts of other discernable movements. As we saw in the last chapter analytic philosophy is a clear and obvious case here. Other such movements in the contemporary stream include phenomenology, existentialism, Critical Theory, poststructuralism, and feminism.

These are not all movements of the same type, and in no case are we dealing with a current of thought with either a sharply defined or a non-overlapping structure. The two points here are worth considering separately. First, we should be clear that none of these movements are monolithic in character, with all or nearly all of the major authors associated with them sharing principles or practices which are everywhere interpreted in the same way. Second, we should be clear that these movements are not everywhere or even usually mutually exclusive. Thus, for example, work which can fairly be regarded as making a contribution to the phenomenological movement – let's say for starters work which has been *explicitly* written in its name – has been produced by authors typically and correctly included as central to the analytic movement. The clearest and most interesting cases here are J. L. Austin[3] and Gilbert Ryle.[4] However, if we lift the restriction and include authors with clear but only *implicit* methodological links and affinities to phenomenological philosophy, then we find that there are a significant number of important analytic philosophers who could be regarded as making a contribution to phenomenology though they do not reach for the title themselves: Stanley Cavell, John McDowell, Hilary Putnam, Cora Diamond and most of the analytic inheritors of Wittgenstein (who – in about 1930 – also took the title for his own work[5]) are obvious candidates.[6]

Nevertheless, just as it is possible to write an introduction to analytic philosophy which pays little attention to its kinships or overlaps with other philosophical movements (and that is typically how such introductions are written), so also it is quite possible to write an introduction to some of the most important contributions to work in phenomenology and mention nothing but works written on mainland Europe (and that is typically how they are written too). On this score, it is worth noting that even if, by restricting oneself in this way, one keeps one's story to the line of greatest dialogical self-sufficiency, one will still not find a methodological monolith. Dermot Moran, one of the best recent introducers of phenomenology (who also restricted himself to geographically Continental authors) begins his study by stressing that 'it is important not to exaggerate . . . the extent to which phenomenology coheres into an agreed method, or accepts one theoretical outlook, or one set of philosophical theses about consciousness, knowledge, and the world'.[7] What is at issue with this movement in the stream is not a series of texts that are tied together by a single shared thread or even a cluster of threads. On the contrary, the phenomenological movement really does *move*: it is characterised less by constant adherence to central principles than by quite radical shifts in subject, method, style and affiliation.[8] So restricting one's attention just to the phenomenologists who are not also analytic philosophers does not reduce the interest one can take in differences within the movement. Nevertheless, if one does let one's view range beyond the Continent one can be newly impressed by the extent to which phenomenology at large includes within it some of the leading figures of the analytic movement. If one takes this on board, and moreover takes on board the extent to which many of the other important currents in the stream of contemporary Western philosophy have in fact taken something from phenomenology, it becomes credible to think that the emergence of the phenomenological movement at large should count as *the* major philosophical event of the past one hundred years of philosophy.

That being said, it is far from being the major event for most philosophy itself in that period. That accolade would go, I think, to the emergence of analytic philosophy, and thus because of its self-discrimination from what it calls 'Continental philosophy' to the emergence of a philosophical culture that has become divided between those who do analytic philosophy and those ('Continental philosophers') who do not. Thus, as we shall see, those philosophers within the analytic movement who took the title of phenomenology for themselves are also among those who (sometimes incredibly) wanted least to do with their European cousins. It is hard not to suspect here a case of what Freud called 'the narcissism of minor differences',[9] and a genuinely comprehensive book on the phenomenological movement would have to include philosophers who belong to the analytic movement as well as those who do not.

But wait! Wouldn't that inclusive undertaking still (if it was honest) have to reproduce within itself the distinction between analytic and

Continental philosophy? While not the same thing, it would certainly be reasonable and interesting to distinguish between phenomenology in the analytic tradition and phenomenology that is not. And, of course, it would be equally reasonable and interesting to distinguish between phenomenology in the Cartesian tradition and phenomenology that is not; and between phenomenology in the existentialist tradition and phenomenology that is not; and between phenomenology in the idealist tradition and phenomenology that is not, and so on. Whether anything reasonable or interesting could be developed by an undertaking which aimed to 'explore' the difference between analytic and Continental phenomenology is, in my view, moot since it begs many questions regarding the functioning of the contrast that would organise it. A central task of this book is to allow us to get clearer on how this distinction really functions – and I hope to show that the chances of decent work being produced on its basis are negligible.

There remain, nevertheless, a number of different ways of pursuing philosophy as phenomenology. However, while it would, as Robert Cumming has noted, be 'silly' to lump them together in a way that elides those differences,[10] one should not ignore the fact that *qua* phenomenologists they are already so 'lumped', and I see no compelling reason not to think of the major proponents (from wherever) as belonging to a distinctive phenomenological movement within the broad stream that comprises the Western inheritance of philosophy. While it overlaps at various points with, or at various points belongs to, other philosophical movements, including especially idealism, existentialism, hermeneutics and postwar analytic philosophy, there is, in my view, no serious distortion in talking about a group of authors whose work is united by the fact that they are all concerned to explore the possibility of inheriting philosophy by doing phenomenology. In other words, to pick up the distinction of the last chapter, the primary texts *of* phenomenology are essentially the primary texts *in* phenomenology too.

Only a Continental philosopher would say that!

I will not here go into the question of what it might mean to 'do phenomenology', not try to explain why one might respond to what calls for philosophy in the first place by pursuing something one wants to call 'phenomenology'. However, since philosophical naturalism is overtaking what Austin called 'linguistic phenomenology' as the dominant mode of analytic philosophy today, it is worth emphasising that one of the most profound points of contact between the major phenomenologists from mainland Europe and the major analytic phenomenologists in the English-speaking world is the shared rejection of the idea that philosophy is either continuous with or is closely affiliated to science, in the sense of the natural sciences. There is good reason to think that the strain of post-Kantian philosophy in which authors such as McDowell and Putnam locate themselves has as much if not more in common with European phenomenology than it does with baldly naturalistic trends in analytic philosophy.

As I have indicated, the writings of Austin, Ryle and Wittgenstein figure centrally to seeing the deep continuities between phenomenology on and phenomenology beyond the European mainland. In his *Introduction to Phenomenology* Moran gives numerous examples which invite such comparisons.[11] Of the many the following will serve as an indication. Against a certain (empiricist) tendency to affirm a preconceptual Given in ordinary experience, the German phenomenologist Martin Heidegger, in lectures from 1925, aimed to affirm that in our practical dealings and engagements we encounter 'things in the environment' (*Umweltding*), a chair, say, and not just 'chair-sensations'. Moran continues the point as follows:

> Hence I can genuinely say 'the chair is uncomfortable' and grasp the mode of being of the chair for me. Abstracting from these practical engagements with the thing makes it an object of theoretical study. At this point, the chair becomes for me a 'natural thing' (*Naturding*) and different epithets apply, for example the chair is made of wood, has such and such a weight, occupies space, and so on. By way of illustration Heidegger says that the botanist studies plants (natural things) not flowers (environmental things), but flowers, not plants, are given as gifts. In 'ordinary speech' (*in der naturlichen Rede*) I say 'I am giving roses', or 'I am giving flowers', but not 'I am giving plants'.[12]

Seeing connections within the phenomenological movement at large helps severely weaken the idea of a distinctive Continental tradition which contrasts markedly (intraphilosophically) with the analytic tradition. There is no plausible way of engaging with the idea of a distinctive Continental tradition which does not acknowledge the centrality of the phenomenological movement to the history of philosophy in Continental Europe in the twentieth century. But it is equally implausible to maintain that this movement has little or nothing in common with central parts of the analytic movement. It would make far more sense to say, as we can see clearly from the wide-angled view, that, strictly speaking, the movement of phenomenology at large *includes* a number of thinkers whose work belongs to the great canonical texts of twentieth century analytic philosophy. As I have mentioned already, some of those thinkers, notably Austin, Ryle and Wittgenstein, were even willing to countenance (admittedly somewhat cautiously) an inheritance of the title for themselves.

Given the connections and proximities seen here, one might think that the idea of the gulf between analytic and Continental philosophy must have emerged with some other movement in view. But that is not so. Bizarre though it may seem, the postwar assumption of a wide gulf between analytic philosophy and Continental philosophy is regularly and almost paradigmatically grasped precisely in terms of the contrast between British philosophical analysis and Continental phenomenology. A basic reason why there is no plausible way of engaging with the idea of a distinctive Continental tradition which does not acknowledge the centrality to it of the phenomenological movement is that for many analytic philosophers during the immediate postwar period 'Continental philosophy' was assumed, on the whole, simply to *be* phenomenology.[13] Other philosophical movements either were not around to figure or, if they were around simply didn't figure on the analytic radar most of the time.[14] This might suggest that there is after all a clear methodological core to the idea of 'Continental philosophy' – namely phenomenology. However, as we have seen, that would not by itself serve to distinguish it in the right kind of way from the analytic movement since parts of that movement also belong to the movement of phenomenology at large. The idea of 'Continental phenomenology' might do the trick, but then it is the addition of the tag 'Continental' that matters. It is the workings of that addition that I am trying to understand in this book.

When Ryle tried to explain the 'wide gulf'[15] between British philosophical analysis and Continental phenomenology he did so on the basis of the difference between a philosophy of concepts which affirms the context principle – a principle which in fact owes more than a passing debt to a European and not a British thinker (Frege)[16] – and a philosophy of concepts which affirms what he identifies as Husserl's Platonist essentialism. This is a significant difference. However, not only would such essentialism be much harder to pin on any phenomenologist (anywhere) after Heidegger, even the contrast between a Fregean and an Husserlian analysis is not as sharply gulf-like as Ryle wanted to suggest. As I mentioned in the last chapter, when Michael

Dummett returned to this Ur-scene of twentieth century philosophy in Europe some forty years later, he saw things very differently:

> At the very beginning of the century, say at the time Husserl published the *Logical Investigations*, there wasn't yet phenomenology as a school. There wasn't yet analytic philosophy as a school. There were lots of currents there and you would have to put Frege and Husserl quite close together, and yet their progeny diverged so widely. It's a very interesting question from which it seems to me that much understanding must come. Why did they diverge so widely?[17]

The early history of the gulf-stricken scene has been revised. But with the assumption that the 'progeny' did 'diverge so widely', Dummett effectively just rejoins Ryle's gulf-seeking rhetoric a little later down the line. The connections that Moran points up between Heidegger's analysis of human existence and ordinary language philosophy (connections the young Ryle may have been a little more willing to identify in his 1928 review of Heidegger's *Being and Time* in *Mind*) pass by without notice. But other authors today have made it possible, without erasing differences, to refocus our perception in more recent texts too. The perception that the progeny of Frege and Husserl 'diverge so widely' is not so evident if one takes a wide-angled view.

What do we see when we take a wide-angled view? Again, even if I can (later) make it seem plausible to regard all the major movements of contemporary Western thought as sharing a common trajectory, the idea is not that we come to see that everything is everywhere really the same. However, by the end of this book I hope two things will have become clear: first, that the most influential reasons and arguments advanced by self-styled *analytic* philosophers for the idea of seeing in the river of Western thought a distinctive Continental current are simply terrible; and, second, that the most influential reasons and arguments advanced by contemporary self-styled *Continental* philosophers for the same idea are also simply terrible. I will not try to advance better arguments to replace them. On the positive side, however, I will try to get us to a stage where we can be reasonably clear why people have gone in for that idea, and what living with or without the title might mean today.

While most of the discussion is negative I will also be providing what I will want to call a *philosophical* (and not merely, say, historical or sociological) account of the emergence of the idea of a 'wide gulf' between the kind of philosophical analysis pursued in the English-speaking world and its Continental Other. As I suggested in the last chapter, the question of 'what philosophy is' is itself a contested concept within the subject we call 'philosophy'. Consequently, insisting that what I am giving will be a *philosophical* account is already a problematic gesture. As soon as anyone starts speaking of something as a 'philosophical account', indeed as soon as someone writes as a philosopher or in the name of philosophy (let's call that the moment of inheritance), anything they say (and the way in which they say it) can always serve simply to reinforce or confirm the well entrenched idea that there are (intraphilosophically) identifiable sides here, and that there are basically only two sides. That is, of everything written in the name of philosophy today, someone might still want to say of it something of the type: 'No/Only (An/A) analytic/Continental philosopher would (never) say that!' For example, someone might say of that sentence: Only a Continental philosopher would say that! So even though I do not want to get caught up in that entrenched idea, I know that these days somewhere along the line I certainly will be, and I want to be able to say and do something about that too. I will address this directly in the last chapter.

Of course, on one way of reading the runes there is no problem identifying two sides here. Making use of the distinction introduced in the last chapter, one could say that you are an analytic philosopher today if your work responds (primarily) to ideas and methods emerging from the primary texts of analytic philosophy, and you are a Continental philosopher today if your work responds (primarily) to ideas and methods emerging from the primary texts of Continental philosophy. However, this symmetry hides a profound dissymmetry. As I see it, and as I hope to show, the fundamental and irreducible feature of the contemporary philosophical culture is the production within the movement of analytic philosophy of a more-or-less stable collection of texts regarded as or encoded as the 'primary works of Continental philosophy'. So the unity one finds on the two sides are of fundamentally different kinds. The unity of analytical philosophy is *a unity of inclusion* based on underlying methodological, thematic and stylistic confluences of the kind identified by Glock. The unity of Continental philosophy, on the other hand, is *a unity of exclusion*, and has no methodological, thematic or stylistic basis at all, broad, loose or otherwise. There is no secret doctrine or hidden principles that will hold them all together in their own right or in their own terms.

Yet we do now have culturally available a fairly stable (if open) list of authors who are usually regarded as 'the major Continental philosophers'. And it will always help students embarking on courses covering some of these thinkers to know who is on that list and to have an idea of what their most significant contribution to philosophy is usually taken to be. I hope to provide a helping hand on this score in the next chapter. The movements in the stream of contemporary philosophy are really quite convoluted and, for most readers from the English-speaking world, reaching out beyond the familiar currents of the analytic movement can feel like being thrown into a particularly disorientating part of that stream. In the last chapter I suggested that there are two responses to that disorientation that I would like to challenge:

1. the response that rationalises that disorientation by identifying work outside the movement of analytic philosophy as belonging to a distinctive Continental tradition;
2. the response that sweeps the problem away by affirming that work in that tradition does not typically represent the most responsible way of going on in philosophy.

As I say, in breaking up the plausibility of the first response I hope also to break up some of the charm of the second. However, while I hope it will lessen the reader's disorientation, it would be a mistake to think that the information I give in the next chapter concerning the work of 'the major Continental philosophers' will help one see why such disorientation gives rise to either of these responses. The kind of brief 'user-friendly' information I hope to give will itself tend merely to cover over the dimension of difficulty or demandingness that the first response is a quite genuine response to. And I have no desire to deny this experienced difficulty.[18] There is no doubt that for many English-speaking readers their first – and often their last – encounter with many of the primary works of Continental philosophy is a miserable one. I take this to be *philosophically* telling. Before turning in the next chapter to some introductory information about them I want to explore this a little further.

Reading the Other

Whether it is often or comfortably acknowledged within the analytic mainstream, there can be no serious doubt that philosophy begins, for all of us, as an inheritance. The idea that one can arrive on the scene and just 'do philosophy', in a vacuum as it were, and in glorious isolation from having had teachers of philosophy is not credible. And that is so even if the learning in question is 'distance learning' because the teacher is in another place or is officially a teacher of another subject or is dead. Acknowledging that philosophy must be inherited invites a more generous interpretation of the fact that students whose path into philosophy comes from a predominantly analytic schooling will find writings which do not belong squarely within that tradition distinctively difficult to read. I will explain this.

As the second response indicates there is a standing option to regard that difficulty as the mark of a distinctive *failure* of the (so-called) Continental tradition: a failure properly to develop arguments and write in competent philosophical prose. However, even those who are drawn into the first response are not obliged to accept the second. Consider Hilary Putnam's explanation of the difficulty analytic philosophers find with the writings of Emmanuel Levinas:

> One reason that analytic philosophers find Levinas hard to read is that he takes it for granted that reading Husserl and Heidegger is part of the education any properly trained philosopher must have just as analytic philosophers take an education which includes reading Russell, Frege, Carnap, and Quine to be what any properly trained philosopher must have.[19]

While I do not accept that it gets to the roots of the demandingness at issue with phenomenological philosophy in general (and so something I think one finds in reading Austin, Ryle and Wittgenstein too), there is clearly something right here. In particular it would surely be a mistake to think that one's own developing philosophical vision is something one could radically separate from what Levinas calls 'the action exercised by the master on me'.[20] As a result one's philosophical schooling is not even notionally separable from the experienced 'legibility' of different texts of philosophy.[21] Samuel Wheeler appeals to this kind of point to redraw an analytic/Continental distinction in a way which affirms the first response but not the second, suggesting 'you are an analytic philosopher if you think Kripke writes clearly, you are a Continental philosopher if you think Heidegger writes clearly'.[22] I don't accept even this way of embracing the distinction, but it serves as a reminder that a philosophical education gives one a distinctive kind of preparation for reading, a preparation that can lead to serious problems when what one is reading does not belong squarely within the purview of that education. What calls out for explanation, however, is why an education in the analytic mainstream prepares one to format alien texts according to the code not only of the first but also of the second response.

Or perhaps I should say: why it used to. While the second response remains powerfully present in the philosophical culture today, there may also be something like a generational shift taking place which is marked by a weakening of ties and a sense that identification with a single movement or style can threaten undue narrowness as well as offer inherited riches. So, for example, not only may more and more analytically trained philosophers feel it worthwhile dipping into writings by one or other or some of 'the major Continental philosophers', they are also more and more likely to have at least one colleague who has spent considerable time studying them closely.[23] Nevertheless, I think what Bernard Williams noted in 1996 remains an unmistakable 'feature of our time': namely, that for many analytically trained readers 'the resources of philosophical writing typically available to analytical philosophy present themselves so strongly as the *responsible* way of going on, the most convincing expression of a philosopher's claim on people's attention'.[24] This is why many people who accept the first response move seamlessly to the second. And there remains a kind of existential bottom line here. As the British logician and epistemologist Timothy Williamson has recently acknowledged, while he would think it 'too crude' to suppose nothing of value is written 'under the aegis of Continental philosophy', he still holds that 'anyone who has taken . . . to heart' the 'philosophical standards' developed within the analytic movement would feel 'a serious loss of integrity' if he or she was to 'participate in Continental philosophy as currently practised'.[25]

No doubt, the thought of such a sober and serious analytic philosopher as Timothy Williamson 'participating in Continental philosophy' is, given the stereotypes, comically incongruous, but there's participation and there's participation, and as Williamson's own rejection of the 'too crude' view indicates, something like philosophical integrity *also* demands that one does not simply close oneself off to writings that do not lie squarely within the scope of one's current field of philosophical vision.

Of course, in my view, what is really 'too crude' is to think that one can make good sense of the idea that there is a distinctively Continental kind of philosophy, a Continental movement or mode or tradition, under whose 'aegis' one might 'go on' in philosophy, well or ill, clearly or unclearly, responsibly or irresponsibly. I'll come back to that again (and again) as we drag ourselves through the story of how it came about that 'Continental philosophy' became the tag for analytic philosophy's hated Other. However, even without that story in view it seems to me evident that there is a rather central dimension of what has been transmitted by (most) teachers of philosophy (everywhere) throughout its long history that itself invites a strongly (negative) evaluative response to philosophical formats that are not congenial to one's acquired philosophical vision. Even if one adheres to the relatively controversial idea that philosophy is ultimately a kind of empirical inquiry (albeit 'at a high level of abstraction') I think that nearly everyone who ends up in one way or another 'doing philosophy' recognises that philosophical investigations are in some sense a priori – that at least some of the 'data' (to use a word that I would love not to see used so much in philosophy) one needs to have in hand in order to get on with philosophical work is something that one already possesses or is, in some way, already to hand.

However, this central and I would think irrecusable dimension of philosophy can make the fact of *teaching* philosophy seem of merely historical or causal interest. The teacher, far from initiating his or her students into a way of going on by introducing something – a form of writing for example – that they do *not* already know, something really *new* to them, is seen only as playing the 'subsidiary function of being midwife to a mind already pregnant with its fruit'.[26] The work of the good philosophy teacher is thus thought to fall by the wayside: the good teacher simply puts one in a good, that is to say autonomously authoritative, position to go on in a way that any (say) 'rational being' is, as such, *in potentia*, already ready to go, and so also to go on disinterestedly to assess the merits of the writings of every other. The student may even feel that he or she is now sensitive to 'philosophical standards' whose worth should be recognisable by any rational being. One should be competent confidently to spot anyone who 'has not learnt his craft'.[27]

While this might explain why we tend to forget the significance of our (ongoing) philosophical education I do not think the shift from the first to the second response can be explained only by this amnesia. For, in principle, one should only be able to spot shortfalls in philosophical standards in a text one *can* read (and justice demands that one *has* actually read it). In the case we are concerned with, however, a certain exasperation or frustration in even making a start leads to what can only be the essentially dogmatic (and thus, I want to say, *philosophically* unsatisfactory) supposition that if 'I, *philosopher*' cannot read the text (it is 'hopelessly unclear') then that itself is a prima facie ground for suspecting some form of (radical) incompetence or some other profound philosophical unhappiness. For this reason the fact that texts that arrive hard to read can rapidly find themselves given a kind of a priori elbow ('I couldn't make any headway at all, it is totally obscure') is no grounds for suspecting radical incompetence. Of course, it is not grounds for suspecting profound philosophical happiness or competence either! But the incontrovertible fact here is that many analytically trained philosophers still think that interest in things 'Continental' is pretty flaky, the upshot of weak minds (or not properly trained minds) finding themselves (perhaps unwittingly and maybe in some ways understandably) caught up in what Austin called the '*ivresse des grande profondeurs*'[28] or captivated by the mystique of prophets and sages. And we need to come to terms with that response in the right way.

The discussion of philosophy as a contested subject should indicate the pointlessness of trying to offer a general defence of those who find their time well spent reading work by (among others) 'the major Continental philosophers'. On the other hand, in my own work I still try to provide an incentive to others to give time where I have found it rewarding myself. I do not regard that as an utterly hopeless ambition. One's education might make one short-sighted but it does not make one entirely blind. It strikes me that one of the reasons why Putnam was able to find his encounter with Levinas a moment of his philosophical education is quite easy to understand. A wide-angled view lets us see that the idea of a gulf between analytic philosophy and Continental philosophy is breached by the very tradition that was supposed to have opened it up. Putnam, already a reader of Austin, Ryle and Wittgenstein, was, in some ways, already well prepared to read Levinas.

Having said that, as I stressed in the last chapter, such points of confluence do not make any of what I will call 'the usual suspects' of Continental philosophy – not even the usual suspects of European phenomenology – merely analytic philosophers with an alternative dress sense. I have no intention of recommending that these writings should henceforth be thought of as assimilable into the analytic tradition.[29] The point is that for many analytic philosophers engaging with such texts makes a peculiar demand: it requires learning to read *other* movements in the philosophical stream otherwise than as one's own *Other*. And so, first and foremost, it requires that one find that the philosophical resources typically available to one provide an only limited competence, or even a structural *in*competence, with regard to these other philosophical resources. And this is what is really so important about a schooling in analytic philosophy with respect to non-analytic resources. The idea of Continental philosophy, the idea that guides the analytic tradition's understanding of such texts, makes available to analytic philosophers a ready fund of distinctions that cannot but lure

Analytic philosophy	The Other of analytic philosophy
Argument	Rhetoric
Logical	Literary
Analysis	Speculation
Clear	Obscure
Rigorous	Vague
Problem-solving	Metaphysical system building
Reason	Passion

Figure 2.1 *Analytic philosophy and its Other.*

its followers towards an endorsement of the second response. Taking a cue from the sort of values identified by Glock in his representation of 'Analytic philosophy at a glance' we can readily construct a table that, by contrast, offers us a specification of its Other (see Figure 2.1).

For reasons I will explain in Chapter 4, the peculiar fate of the idea of Continental philosophy was to become the Other of analytic philosophy. But for just these reasons reading the texts that are identified as 'the primary works of Continental philosophy' with any rigour (that is, as other than analytic philosophy's own Other) will require that readers with a background only in analytic philosophy be able to place themselves and their sense of philosophical competence in question. That is obviously a huge demand for any reader. For many, no doubt, too huge. If one allows one's competence to be open to question here one is faced with an apparently endless series of further questions. How should one begin to go about responding to these other texts? Where should one begin? What standards should one bring to the texts one reads? And so on. I do not know how to answer these questions except concretely, except by inviting readers to let the texts they are reading prepare them anew. There is no doubt that readers who are determined to 'believe they really are philosophers and know what philosophy is and how to do it' will not get very far.[30] I will have got somewhere, however, if any reader of this book learns to find the idea of belonging comfortably to a philosophical fold a matter for further philosophical scrutiny.

Notes

1. David West, *An Introduction to Continental Philosophy*, Oxford: Polity, 1996, p. 1.
2. Hilary Putnam, cited from an interview, in John McCumber, *Time in the Ditch*, Evanston, IL: Northwestern University Press, 2001, p. 50.

3. 'I think it might be better to use, for this way of doing philosophy, some less misleading name than those given above – for instance "linguistic phenomenology", only that is rather a mouthful' (J. L. Austin, 'A Plea for Excuses', in *Philosophical Papers*, Oxford: Clarendon, 1979, p. 182).

4. 'Though it is entitled *The Concept of Mind*, it is actually an examination of multifarious specific mental concepts . . . The book could be described as a sustained essay in phenomenology, if you are at home with that label' (Gilbert Ryle, 'Phenomenology versus *The Concept of Mind*', in *Collected Papers*, London: Hutchinson, 1971, p. 188).

5. 'You could say of my work that it is "phenomenology"' (Ludwig Wittgenstein, in *Recollections of Wittgenstein*, ed. Rush Rhees, Oxford: OUP, 1984, p. 116).

6. Although they are *far* less shy about their indebtedness to and affinity with non-analytic studies in phenomenology, it should also be noted that there is also a very lively and influential approach in cognitive science, known as 'the embodied mind', which carries phenomenological philosophy into the heart of present-day analytic concerns in the philosophy of mind. The most important contributions here are from Hubert Dreyfus, Andy Clark and Francisco Varela.

7. Dermot Moran, *Introduction to Phenomenology*, London: Routledge, 2000, p. 3.

8. The best place to see this movement move is in Robert Denoon Cumming's four-volume study *Phenomenology and Deconstruction*, Chicago: Chicago University Press, 1991–2001.

9. The phrase is cited (without an identifying reference) by Timothy Garton Ash in *Free World*, London: Allen Lane, 2004, p. 183.

10. Robert Denoon Cumming, 'Role-playing: Sartre's Transformation of Husserl's Phenomenology', in *Cambridge Companion to Sartre*, ed. C. Howells, Cambridge: CUP, 1992, p. 42.

11. *Understanding Phenomenology* (R. Keat et al., Oxford: Blackwell, 1980) also makes many helpful comparisons, particularly to Ryle and Wittgenstein.

12. Dermot Moran, *Introduction to Phenomenology*, p. 232.

13. This identification of phenomenology with Continental philosophy is evident in Dummett's discussion of the two streams having their origins in Frege and Husserl (see below).

14. I am grateful to discussions with John Sellars for bringing home to me the significance of this, and for drawing my attention to the current University of London syllabus which still more or less identifies what it calls 'Continental philosophy' with Continental European phenomenology.

15. Gilbert Ryle, 'Phenomenology versus *The Concept of Mind*', p. 182.

16. Since he is trying to maintain a kind of British philosophical purism of the analytic movement Ryle stumbles over this debt to Frege. He retains it with the finesse that on the Continent 'logical theory' has been studied and developed not by philosophers at all but only by 'a few departments of mathematics' ('Phenomenology versus *The Concept of Mind*', p. 182). I will come back to this in Chapter 4.

17. Michael Dummett, in an interview with Fabrice Pataut, *Philosophical Investigations*, vol. 19, no. 1, 1996, p. 14.
18. In the case of writings in phenomenology I believe that a certain experienced difficulty *should* belong to anyone's engagement with them. See Simon Glendinning, 'What is Phenomenology?' *Think*, no. 7, 2004, pp. 33–41.
19. Hilary Putnam, 'Levinas and Judaism', in *The Cambridge Companion to Levinas*, eds S. Critchley and R. Bernasconi, Cambridge: CUP, 2002, p. 40.
20. Emmanuel Levinas, *Totality and Infinity*, Pittsburgh: Duquesne University Press, 1969, p. 99.
21. The idea of a conceptual component not being 'notionally separable' from experience is John McDowell's way of making a central thought in Kant vivid. I am deliberately borrowing that thought here.
22. Samuel Wheeler III, *Deconstruction as Analytic Philosophy*, Stanford, CA: Stanford University Press, 2000, p. 2.
23. See the Appendix for statistical details on this in the British context.
24. Bernard Williams, 'Contemporary Philosophy: A Second Look', in *The Blackwell Companion to Philosophy*, eds N. Bunnin and E. P. Tsui-James, Oxford: Blackwell, p. 27, italics mine.
25. Timothy Williamson, *New British Philosophy: The Interviews*, p. 151.
26. Emmanuel Levinas, *Totality and Infinity*, p. 98.
27. R. M. Hare, 'A School for Philosophers', *Ratio*, vol. 11, no. 2, 1969, pp. 112–13.
28. J. L. Austin, 'A Plea for Excuses', p. 179.
29. Stella Sanford interprets the implicit direction of my argument against the idea of a distinctive Continental tradition in this way in her essay 'Johnny Foreigner' (*Radical Philosophy*, no. 102, 2000, p. 43), but as I am trying to make clearer in this book this is not what I am up to at all.
30. Geoffrey Bennington, 'For the Sake of Argument (Up to a Point)', in *Arguing with Derrida*, ed. S. Glendinning, Oxford: Blackwell, 2001, p. 38.

3

The Usual Suspects

Caveat Emptor (Buyer Beware)

The engagement with texts outside the mainstream of analytic philosophy that has characterised my own work in philosophy has always involved an effort indirectly to intervene in the regular programming of analytic expectations about such texts. By rendering myself capable of reading these texts I have sought to encourage others to feel less well prepared for what they might encounter. My thought is that without such a disruption they will remain prepared only for the (for them, for everyone) depressing prospect of reading the Other.[1]

As I will explain in the next chapter, such preparatory expectations express a deep and very important commitment on the part of analytic philosophers to distinctive and demanding standards of rigour and clarity. But in the assumption that there is a tradition which is marked precisely by its *failure* to cherish such standards these preparatory expectations are quite useless for reading works that do not belong to the analytic mainstream – at least not with any rigour or clarity. So they need disrupting. Readers need to experience their competence at reading every other as questionable, and need to find it seriously too crude to close down their own capacity to follow other steps. One of the most continuously disruptive, disquieting and difficult writers in the line up of the usual suspects of Continental philosophy, Jacques Derrida, sums up his fears with regard to his readers in the following passage:

> Because I still like him, I can foresee the impatience of the *bad* reader: this is the way I name or accuse the fearful reader, the reader in a hurry to be determined, decided upon deciding (in order to annul, in other words to bring back to oneself, one has to wish to know in advance what to expect, one wishes to expect what has happened, one wishes to expect (oneself)). Now, it is bad, and I know of no other definition of the bad, it is bad to predestine one's reading, it is always bad to foretell. It is bad, reader, no longer to like retracing one's steps.[2]

Derrida retains the hope that his readers will not dive headlong into pre-programmed assumptions with regard to what they might find in a supposedly 'deconstructionist' text.[3] However, everyone who has found their time well spent with texts that do not lie squarely in the mainstream of analytic philosophy will know how hopeless that hope often is. Nevertheless, because I still like analytic philosophers I want to disrupt their tendency to get too quickly, sometimes immediately, caught up in what I have identified as the two basic responses to the difficulty they find engaging with texts that do not lie squarely within their home horizons:

1. the response that rationalises that difficulty by identifying such work as belonging to a distinctive 'Continental tradition';
2. the response that sweeps the problem of reading away by affirming that work in that tradition does not typically represent the most responsible way of going on in philosophy

In this book I want directly to engage with the first response in order indirectly to disrupt the second.[4] So without providing the kind of (I hope) careful reading of texts that would normally allow me indirectly to intervene in the normative programming of the second response, I still regard it as possible to do so. As I see it there are two other ways in which one may go about this. First, one can look at arguments or reasons for affirming the idea of such a Continental tradition, and try to show that the inferior quality of the arguments and reasons calls into question the very idea of it. That is what I will be doing in the two chapters following this one. Alternatively, one can get a sense of the implausibility of the first response by achieving an overview of the motley included within this supposed tradition. One can, in this way, get a vivid sense of what radically discredits that response: namely, the fact that what is getting grouped together as the primary works in Continental philosophy 'is a highly eclectic and disparate series of intellectual currents that could hardly be said to amount to a unified tradition'.[5] This is the path I will follow in this chapter: giving an overview of the authors of what we can sensibly (if not particularly happily) conceive as the primary texts of Continental philosophy, an overview of what I am calling the usual suspects.

My aim in this overview is therefore exactly the opposite of the standard one of giving (even the beginnings of) an introduction to a philosophical tradition, its major thinkers and their thoughts. And to further this fundamentally non-standard end a number of things should be borne in mind as we proceed. First and foremost it is important to stress that I am not attempting to undermine confidence in the idea of a distinctive Continental tradition of philosophy in order to suggest that the authors usually included in it can and should henceforth be assimilated into the analytic tradition. Of course, I do not want to suggest that they can or should be grasped as belonging to the Other of that tradition either. They are not, for example, philosophical approaches *hostile* to rigour or clarity. Nevertheless, they may well be approaches which (in various ways) question assumptions in analytic philosophy's understanding of what it is to possess those characteristics, assumptions which bear on what we should regard as 'the most convincing expression of a philosopher's claim on people's attention'.[6] This is why coming to terms with these (in various ways) genuinely other philosophical resources cannot but involve analytically trained readers learning to find their own philosophical resources as an obstacle rather than an interpretive aid in reading such texts. As I have noted, this gives rise to a serious problem for uninitiated readers concerning how to begin taking steps reading these other texts. And the second point I want to emphasise is that the overview that follows is not intended even to begin to resolve that problem. The only systematic answer I can give in this book to that problem is that a serious contribution to philosophy will itself offer guidance to becoming a reader of that contribution.

The overview I will present has the form of a listing of proper names in historical sequence. There is an irony to making use of this format, for there is an old joke that suggests that the distinction between analytic and Continental philosophy principally resides in the fact that the former deals with 'problems' and the latter deals with 'proper names'.[7] Simon Critchley was forced to confront this caricature in defence of the 'principle of selection' for his own *Companion to Continental Philosophy*, a principle that was precisely one of 'organizing the *Companion* by proper names'.[8] Critchley's defence was that, caricatures aside, this principle is not appropriate only to one side of the supposed divide. On the contrary, the 'easiest and most minimal' way of distinguishing analytic and Continental philosophy is, he suggested, 'on both sides' through proper names: 'what matters here is which tradition the philosopher feels part of, knowing who counts (and perhaps more importantly, knowing who doesn't count – sometimes without knowing why) as an ancestor or an authority, who's in and who's out'.[9]

Critchley's sense of 'what matters' here should ring true for anyone thinking about their own involvement in a tradition. Consequently, we might think we can now simply ask those who feel part of the Continental tradition to specify who is 'in' as far as they are concerned. But Critchley's somewhat cautious parenthetical point about it 'perhaps' being 'more important' knowing who is 'out' should not, in my view, be passed over so quickly, nor mentioned so cautiously and parenthetically, especially in this case. If we are to take seriously the interpretive proposals set out in Chapter 1 then we must also take seriously something implicitly invited by the cautious parenthetical note: namely, that in the case of the Continental collection we are dealing with a set whose unity is originally *forged by exclusion*. What if the set is originally formed from thinkers who are typically regarded as 'out' by (self-authorised) analytic philosophers?[10] So in addition to the points already mentioned, as we approach the overview of the usual suspects we must not lose sight of the possibility (a possibility that I think is actual) that as a list, precisely, of 'the major Continental philosophers' it has its roots in analytic philosophy's movement of self-differentiation, and is composed precisely of those thinkers who have come to be regarded as 'out'. We must hold fast too to Critchley's thought that individual philosophers may not know *why* someone counts as 'out' in their tradition. And finally we must remember as well that there is no earthly reason why any one of the names that figure in the list we are about to look at might not figure in the list of those who are cited as an ancestor or an authority for particular philosophers who feel or declare themselves as belonging to the analytic tradition. (Many of them will have been whether they have read them or not.) With all that in mind, I will now present something like an 'A' list (by date of birth) of 'the major Continental philosophers' (and the major not-simply-philosophical comrades who they care about) since Kant.[11]

An 'A' list of Continental Philosophers

Kant, Immanuel (1724–1804), German philosopher, almost universally ranked as the most important thinker of modern times. The keystone of Kant's 'critical philosophy', his transcendental idealism, is presented in his *Critique of Pure Reason* (1781, revised 1787; trans. 1855), also known as the First Critique. The central idea of Kant's idealism is that the structure

. . .

41

of objectivity of all objects of experience (spatio-temporal particulars in nature) has its source in the structure of subjectivity, in a priori conditions for the unity of subjective representations. Kant's ethical ideas, in particular his conception of human beings as worthy of unconditional respect, are the outcome of his belief in the fundamental freedom of the individual as stated in his *Critique of Practical Reason* (1788; trans. 1879), also known as the Second Critique. In the *Critique of Judgement* (1790; trans. 1928), also known as the Third Critique, Kant attempts to construct a bridge between the faculties of the understanding (whose concern is knowledge of nature) and reason (whose concern is freedom). Specifically, it deals with the capacity to make aesthetic and teleological judgements.

Fichte, Johann Gottlieb (1762–1814), German philosopher. Fichte was a proponent of an idealist theory of reality and moral action and, along with Friedrich Schelling and G. W. F. Hegel, was one of the most important figures in the philosophical movement of German idealism. In Fichte's view, we can either try to explain consciousness in terms of the activity of the objective world upon human beings or explain the objective world in terms of the activity of consciousness. Fichte argued that only the second option is compatible with human freedom. Fichte's works include *The Science of Knowledge* (1794; trans. 1970), *The Science of Rights* (1796; trans. 1869), *The Science of Ethics as Based on the Science of Knowledge* (1798; trans. 1907) and *Addresses to the German Nation* (1808; trans. 1922). His most accessible work, introducing his basic ideas in deliberately plain and simple language, is *The Vocation of Man* (1800; trans. 1956).

Schleiermacher, Friedrich Daniel Ernst (1768–1834), German theologian, who is often called the father of the hermeneutic tradition. Hermeneutics is defined by Schleiermacher as the 'art of understanding' where its object is any 'foreign' or 'strange' discourse that aims to communicate thoughts. The crucial point here is that understanding in this case presupposes a development of one's understanding. His greatest contribution on this subject, published under the title *Hermeneutics: The Handwritten Manuscripts* (1977), was constantly reworked by Schleiermacher but never prepared for publication.

Hegel, Georg Wilhelm Friedrich (1770–1831), German philosopher, who became one of the most influential thinkers of the nineteenth century, and the self-appointed apogee of German idealism. A major feature of Hegel's writing is his interest in the philosophy of history and the history of philosophy. Almost all Hegel scholars accept that, for Hegel, historical

. . .

considerations are integral to his philosophical concerns and were not items tacked on to some non-historically conceived approach to philosophy. *The Phenomenology of Spirit* (1807; trans. 1910) is usually thought to be his most important work. Hegel published over a period of several years *The Science of Logic* (1812, 1813, 1816; trans. 1929). In 1817 he published in summary form a systematic statement of his entire philosophy entitled *Encyclopedia of the Philosophical Sciences in Outline* (1817 rev. edn 1827, 1830; trans. 1959). The last full-length work published by Hegel was *The Philosophy of Right* (1821; trans. 1896), although several sets of his lecture notes, supplemented by students' notes, were published after his death.

Schelling, Friedrich Wilhelm Joseph von (1775–1854), German philosopher, and one of the leading figures in the movement of German idealism. Throughout his career Schelling sought an equilibrium between the demand for a theoretical system, which ties him to the rationalist metaphysicians of the eighteenth century, and the demand for freedom, through which he anticipates the emergence of existentialism. It has also been suggested that the shape of argument in Derrida's 'deconstruction' bears striking similarities to those found in Schelling's writings. Schelling's many works include *System of Transcendental Idealism* (1800; trans. 1978), *Ideas for a Philosophy of Nature* (1803; trans. 1988), *Of Human Freedom* (1809; trans. 1936) and *On the History of Modern Philosophy* (1827; trans. 1994).

Schopenhauer, Arthur (1788–1860), German philosopher. While mercilessly hostile to German idealism, Schopenhauer's work is deeply Kantian in character, based on the duality of appearances and thing-in-itself, a duality mirrored in the fundamental dualism of his 'system', that of world as representation and world as will. Unlike Kant, however, he did not regard the thing-in-itself to be in principle beyond every possible experience. On the contrary, it is given in 'inner' experience of one's own will. His principal work, *The World as Will and Representation* (1819; trans. 1883), outlines his distinctive appropriation of Kant's dualism and presents an account of the essential unity of metaphysics, ethics and aesthetics.

Feuerbach, Ludwig Andreas (1804–72), German philosopher, who appealed to principles of psychology to explain orthodox religious belief and developed one of the first German materialistic philosophies. Feuerbach was a pupil of Hegel's. While deeply indebted to Hegel, Feuerbach's philosophy is characterised by its rejection of Hegel's abstract idealism. Feuerbach's call for a 'new basis of things' was intended to restore

. . .

real significance to 'man and his world'. In his chief work, *The Essence of Christianity* (1841; trans. 1854), Feuerbach stated that the existence of religion is justifiable only in that it satisfies a psychological need: a person's essential preoccupation is with the self, and the worship of God is actually worship of an idealised self.

Kierkegaard, Søren Aabye (1813–55), Danish philosopher, whose concern with individual existence, choice and commitment profoundly influenced modern existentialism. Many of his works were originally published under pseudonyms. He applied the term 'existential' to his work because he regarded philosophy as the expression of an intensely examined individual life, not as the construction of a monolithic system in the manner of Hegel, whose work he attacked in *Concluding Unscientific Postscript* (1846; trans. 1941). In his first major work, *Either/Or* (2 vols, 1843; trans. 1944), Kierkegaard described two 'stages' of existence: the aesthetic and the ethical. In his later works, such as *Stages on Life's Way* (1845; trans. 1940), Kierkegaard proposed a third stage, the religious, in which one submits to the will of God, but in so doing finds authentic freedom. In *Fear and Trembling* (1843; trans. 1941) Kierkegaard focused on God's command that Abraham sacrifice his son Isaac. Other major writings include *The Concept of Anxiety* (1844; trans. 1944), *The Present Age* (1846; trans. 1940) and *The Sickness unto Death* (1849; trans. 1941).

Marx, Karl (1818–83), German political philosopher and revolutionary, co-founder with Friedrich Engels of scientific socialism and, as such, one of the most influential thinkers in modern history. In 1847 Marx and Engels were commissioned to formulate a statement of socialist principles. The programme they submitted was *The Communist Manifesto* (1848; trans. 1888) The central propositions of the Manifesto embody the neo-Hegelian theory, later explicitly formulated in his *Critique of Political Economy* (1859; trans. 1904), called the dialectical materialist conception of history, or historical materialism. *The Economic and Philosophical Manuscripts* (written 1844, first pub. 1932; trans. 1959) is perhaps Marx's most influential philosophical contribution, but his greatest work of political philosophy and economy is undoubtedly *Capital* (vol. 1, 1867; vols 2 and 3, edited by Engels and published posthumously in 1885 and 1894, respectively; trans. 1907–09).

Dilthey, Wilhelm (1833–1911), German philosopher of history and culture, whose theories have especially influenced theology and sociology. Dilthey saw himself as heir to Kant's critical philosophy, and conceived his life's work as a Critique of Historical Reason. That is, where Kant provided an

. . .

epistemological foundation for the natural sciences, Dilthey aimed to establish the epistemological foundations for those disciplines concerned with meaning, value and purpose: what he called the 'human sciences'. Dilthey's hermeneutic theory of historical understanding was presented in a number of books, and in greatest detail in *The Formation of the Historical World in the Human Sciences* (1910; trans. 1976).

Nietzsche, Friedrich Wilhelm (1844–1900), German philosopher, and one of the most provocative thinkers of the modern period. His influence has been all pervasive, most obviously in his pronouncement of the death of God; his 'aristocratic' critique of traditional and specifically Christian morality of 'good and evil' as a 'slave' morality; his diagnosis of modernity in terms of its 'nihilism'; and his call for 'a transvaluation of all values'. A prolific writer, he wrote several major works, among them *The Birth of Tragedy* (1872; trans. 1967), *Daybreak* (1881; trans. 1974), *The Gay Science* (1882; trans. 1974), *Thus Spoke Zarathustra* (1883–85; trans. 1961), *Beyond Good and Evil* (1886; trans. 1973), *On the Genealogy of Morals* (1887; trans. 1967), *The Antichrist* (1895; trans. 1968), *Ecce Homo* (1908; trans. 1968) and the controversially edited notes published posthumously as *The Will to Power* (1901; trans. 1910).

Brentano, Franz (1838–1917), German philosopher and psychologist. In 1874 Brentano published his most famous work, *Psychology from an Empirical Standpoint* (1874; trans. 1973). In the same year he became a teacher in Vienna. Among the students present at his lectures were Sigmund Freud and Edmund Husserl. He is often called the father of phenomenology. Brentano is most famous for his 'intentionality' thesis: 'Every mental phenomenon is characterised by what the Scholastics of the Middle Ages called the intentional (or mental) inexistence of an object'. 'Inexistence' here does not mean 'non-existence' but 'existence within the mind'. The thesis thus asserts that all conscious phenomenon are characterised by their being a consciousness *of* some mental content: a contentful mental accusative is always included within the description of any mental act.

Cohen, Hermann (1842–1918), German-Jewish philosopher, and one of the founders of the Neo-Kantian school at Marburg. He was probably the most important Jewish philosopher of the nineteenth century although his major works are purely secular. Cohen's commentaries on Kant, written over some forty years, notably his *Kant's Theorie der Erfahrung* [Kant's Theory of Experience] (1871), helped to established Marburg as a world centre for Neo-Kantian studies. His studies in ethics and religion affirmed

. . .

Kant's claim that ethics had to be universal, an affirmation that Cohen interpreted in terms of our striving (infinitely) towards a goal of complete social justice. His emphasis on Judaism's universal ethics developed into a systematic conception of 'ethical monotheism' that has influenced many Jewish and religious philosophers.

Freud, Sigmund (1856–1939), Austrian physician and founder of psychoanalysis. His hugely influential book *The Interpretation of Dreams* was first published in 1900 (trans. 1911). Freud's work effected a radical complication or 'decentring' of both classical and everyday psychology. Freud claims that ordinary actions are typically determined by networks of motives far more extensive and complex that we normally realise or are aware of. There are parts of ourselves that we have a relation to akin to that which we have to others. According to Freud, many everyday desires arise, in part, from motives which are unconscious residues of encounters with significant persons and situations from the past, reaching back into infancy.

Saussure, Ferdinand de (1857–1913), Swiss linguist. Saussure is best known for his *Course in General Linguistics* (1916; trans. 1959), a text which was constructed from his lecture notes and other materials after his death. He is often called the father of structuralism. Saussure made explicit the implications of a structuralist approach to language which claims that language is a system of differences, not a collection of word-atoms or other 'positive terms'. He made a series of theoretical distinctions which became the foundation of structuralist linguistics, for example between *langue* (the system of language) and *parole* (events of speech), and a conception of the sign as a two-sided unity comprised of a signifier (acoustic image) and a signified (concept).

Bergson, Henri (1859–1941), French philosopher. Bergson is probably best known for his 'vitalism', an evolutionary and deeply biological theory of knowledge and the intellect. His theory tends to favour natural instincts 'moulded on the very form of life' over the intellect. The latter is, he says, 'characterised by a natural inability to comprehend life'. Emmanuel Levinas recalls that during the prewar period, and particularly during the 1920s, Bergson '*was* philosophy' in France. Bergson's thought is contained in four major books: *Time and Free Will* (1889; trans. 1910), *Matter and Memory* (1897; trans. 1911), *Creative Evolution* (1907; trans. 1911), *The Two Sources of Morality and Religion* (1932; trans. 1935) and two smaller books: *Laughter* (1937; trans. 1911) and *Duration and Simultaneity* (1921; trans. 1922). Two books of collected essays were also published: *Mind Energy* (1919; trans. 1920) and *An Introduction to Metaphysics: The Creative Mind* (1934; trans. 1946).

Husserl, Edmund (1859–1938), German philosopher, and official inaugurator of phenomenology. His first book, *Philosophy of Arithmetic* (1891; trans. 2003) was roundly criticised by Frege for its supposed 'psychologism', and his mature writings, beginning with the *Logical Investigations* (1900–01; trans. 1970), are far more clearly resistant to that charge. The Fifth Logical Investigation is famous for introducing the notion of intentionality (with explicit reference to Brentano) as central to the understanding of consciousness and mental content. His later writings develop within a point of view greatly indebted to but also distinctively critical of Descartes and Kant. His major works of such 'transcendental phenomenology' are *Ideas: A General Introduction to Pure Phenomenology* (1913; trans. 1931), *Cartesian Meditations* (1931; trans. 1960) and *The Crisis of European Sciences and Transcendental Phenomenology. An Introduction to Phenomenological Philosophy* (1934–37; trans. 1970).

Rickert, Heinrich (1863–1936), German philosopher, one of the leading Neo-Kantians and a crucial figure in discussion of the foundations of the social sciences in the early twentieth century. He endorses a rigorous distinction between natural science and historical science, but he does not follow Dilthey in arguing that the difference is grounded in differences between two kinds of material or modes of existence. The difference is rather one of *'logical* structure' or mode of conceptualisation: between conceptualisations which are remote from empirical reality itself in virtue of aiming at its general laws (natural science) and those which are interested in certain individual and concrete qualities of empirical reality (historical science). Rickert's most important work is *The Limits of Concept Formation in Natural Science* (1902, trans. 1986).

Cassirer, Ernst (1874–1945), German philosopher, born in Poland. A great admirer of Kant's critical philosophy, Cassirer was a leading figure in the Marburg Neo-Kantian school. Cassirer conceived human beings as inhabiting their environment in a radically original way in virtue of their uses of symbolic systems and symbolic forms. This use of symbols 'transforms the whole of human life. As compared with the other animals man lives not merely in a broader reality; he lives, so to speak, in a new *dimension* of reality'. Cassirer's works include *The Philosophy of Symbolic Forms* (3 vols, 1923–29; trans. 1955–57), *The Logic of the Humanities* (1942; trans. 1961) and *The Problem of Knowledge* (1950).

Buber, Martin (1878–1965), German-Jewish philosopher, who developed a philosophy of encounter, or dialogue. His most widely known work, *I and*

. . .

Thou (1922; trans. 1937), is a concise expression of his philosophy. A crucial forerunner of Levinas, Buber views human existence in terms of two fundamental kinds of relation: 'I-It' and 'I-Thou' relations. I-It relations comprise those taken up by a human being with things in the world. The I-Thou relation, by contrast, is the relation in which a human being enters into a meeting, through dialogue, with another person. Of his other major works, *On Judaism* (1923; trans. 1967) established his intellectual importance to the German-Jewish community.

Hartmann, Nicolai (1882–1950), German philosopher and one of the central figures in the Marburg Neo-Kantian school. For Hartmann metaphysical problems are those which form the horizon of scientific knowledge, and which are inescapable because of their connection with what we can know scientifically, yet which cannot be solved by the methods of science alone. Like other figures in the Marburg school he was particularly concerned to criticise the tendency to employ categories or principles from one region or province to another that differs from it in kind, for example the application of mechanistic principles to the sphere of the organic, of organic relationships to social and political life, and, conversely, of mental and spiritual structures to the inanimate world. His major works include *Ethics* (1926; trans. 1932), *Der Aufbau der realen Welt* (1940) and *New Ways of Ontology* (1943; trans. 1952).

Jaspers, Karl (1883–1969), German philosopher and psychologist, one of the originators of modern existentialism. Jaspers used the term 'Existenz' to designate the fundamental character of our being that grounds our presence in the world, and regarded his philosophy as a work of the clarification of Existenz. Jaspers also wrote extensively on the threat to human freedom posed by modern science and modern economic and political institutions. His major works include *General Psychopathology* (1913; trans. 1963), *Psychology of World Views* (1919) and *Philosophy and Existence* (1938; trans. 1971).

Lukács, Georg (1885–1971), Hungarian Marxist philosopher. Lukács's major writings on literature and philosophy incorporate ideas from the German sociologist Max Weber into traditional Marxist analyses. He is best known for his book *History and Class Consciousness* (1923; trans. 1967). This book was to influence many later Marxists and critical theorists, particularly its discussion of alienation.

Bloch, Ernst (1885–1977), German philosopher and social theorist. Somewhat misleadingly regarded as part of the movement of Critical Theory,

. . .

Bloch's work incorporates elements of Hegelian Marxism, phenomenology, literary expressionism, Kierkegaardian existentialism, hermeneutics, secular-theological utopianism and a Schelling-influenced philosophy of nature. His work spans the period from 1919, when he published *Spirit of Utopia*, to 1974 when he wrote his last major book *Experimentum Mundi*. Other major works include *The Principle of Hope* (1954), *Atheism in Christianity* (1968) and *Natural Law and Human Dignity* (1961).

Heidegger, Martin (1889–1976), German philosopher, who developed a radically new form of phenomenology, and is widely regarded as one of the most original philosophers of the twentieth century. His most important and influential work (though unfinished) is *Being and Time* (1927; trans. 1962). Fundamental to Heidegger's thought is his claim that the meta-physical tradition fails to do justice to the 'ontological difference', to the difference, that is, between entities (beings) and the Being of entities. *Being and Time* is dominated by an analysis of the Being of the entity that can grasp (or fail to grasp) this difference: the entity that we ourselves are, and which Heidegger calls *Dasein*. His numerous later writings explore, among many other topics, questions concerning art and technology, and the idea of the end of philosophy.

Marcel, Gabriel (1889–1973), French Roman Catholic existentialist philosopher, who insisted that individuals can only be understood as embodied and involved in specific situations. Marcel proposes a funda-mental distinction between the body as something possessed (like property or equipment) and the body as something that one is: a distinction between 'having' and 'being' a body. Marcel was also concerned that scientific think-ing, with its reductionism and technicality, avoids the mystery of life in favour of 'problems' and 'solutions'. His ideas are developed in a number of books, including *Being and Having* (1935; trans. 1965), *The Mystery of Being* (1950; trans. 1950) *Creative Fidelity* (1940; trans. 1964) and *Tragic Wisdom and Beyond* (1969; trans. 1973).

Gramsci, Antonio (1891–1937), Italian Marxist thinker and activist, one of the founders of the Italian Communist party. Developing traditional Marxist ideas on ideology, Gramsci's influence has continued through his *Prison Notebooks* (1948–51; trans. 1971).

Benjamin, Walter (1892–1940), German writer, Marxist theorist and aes-thetician. Closely identified with (but not a member of) the Frankfurt School, Benjamin is best known for his essays 'The Work of Art in the Age

. . .

49

of Mechanical Reproduction' in *Illuminations* (1931; trans. 1968), and 'The Author as Producer', (1934; trans. 1966). His oeuvre comprises writings in philosophy, literary and art criticism, political theory and theology.

Horkheimer, Max (1895–1973), Jewish-German philosopher and social theorist, Director of the Institute for Social Research in Frankfurt ('the Frankfurt School') and inaugurator of the 'Critical Theory' of society. The basic feature of Critical Theory is the refusal absolutely to separate fact from value. It understands that all theoretical projects, including its own, necessarily serve, and are shaped by, social interests and exist in particular social contexts. However, for Horkheimer Critical Theory is to be distinguished from sceptical relativism by its insistence on the possibility of sustaining truth claims. See entry on Adorno for major publication details.

Marcuse, Herbert (1898–1979), German-American philosopher, closely identified with (but not a member of) the Frankfurt School. His social philosophy is outlined in *Eros and Civilization* (1955) and *One-Dimensional Man* (1964). One of the most distinctive aspects of Marcuse's work is the extent to which it embodies a distinctively reciprocal reception of Heidegger's phenomenology and of Marx's historical materialism.

Gadamer, Hans-Georg (1900–2002), German philosopher. In his development of a philosophical hermeneutics in his major work *Truth and Method* (1960; trans. 1975), Gadamer claims to follow his former teacher Heidegger in conceiving understanding as 'the basic motion' of our existence. The idea here is that understanding is not essentially a theoretical posture that we might try to achieve or adopt now and then, but is something that belongs to what we 'are' all the time. However, according to Gadamer this structure of being cannot be reduced to a technique or a set of rules: it is, as Schleiermacher said, an 'art', one connected to knowledge but not accounted for by the idea of method. Among his other numerous books and collections are *Philosophical Hermeneutics* (3 vols 1967–72; trans. 1976), *The Relevance of the Beautiful and Other Essays* (1967 and 1977; trans. 1986) and *Reason in the Age of Science* (1976; trans. 1982).

Lacan, Jacques (1901–81), French psychoanalyst. Lacan's major volume of writings, *Ecrits* (1966; trans. 1977) is famous for providing a structuralist reading of Freudian theory. His most significant thesis concerns the importance of understanding language to understanding the workings of the unconscious. He bases his account on the fact that Freud's theory of the two main mechanisms of unconscious processes, condensation and

. . .

displacement, can be expressed as linguistic transformations: where meaning is either condensed (in metaphor) or displaced (in metonymy). Adopting ideas from Saussure, Lacan argues that the unconscious is 'structured like a language'. Other important collections of Lacan's seminars include *The Four Fundamental Concepts of Psychoanalysis* (1973; trans 1977) and *The Ethics of Psychoanalysis* (1986; trans. 1992).

Adorno, Theodor Wiesengrund (1903–69), German philosopher and social theorist. Most closely associated with the Frankfurt School, although he did not become a member until the 1940s. In 1938 he emigrated to the United States, where he worked with Horkheimer on *Dialectic of Enlightenment* (1947; trans. 1972) and other books. Adorno and Horkheimer returned to teaching in Frankfurt in 1951. Articulated in terms of a Marxist account of society, the central concern of Adorno's philosophy is the problem of how to think about (and engage with) the world in a culture that inhibits critical reflection on, and conceptualisation of, that world. His key publications after the war include *Minima Moralia* (1951; trans. 1974), *The Jargon of Authenticity* (1964; trans. 1973) and *Negative Dialectics* (1966; trans. 1973).

Sartre, Jean-Paul (1905–80), French philosopher, writer and leading exponent of modern existentialism. In 1938 he published his philosophical novel *Nausea* (trans. 1949) and in 1943 he published a play, *The Flies* (trans. 1946), as well as his major philosophical work *Being and Nothingness* (trans. 1953). That work sets out to develop a rigorously anti-phenomenalist phenomenology of 'human reality'. Some of his more accessible 'existentialist' views were popularised in *Existentialism and Humanism* (1946; trans. 1948). Sartre's later philosophical work *Critique of Dialectical Reason* (1960; trans. 1976) shifted his emphasis from individual freedom to a Marx-influenced theory of the subject as an actor who is always historically and socially conditioned. Sartre's other main works include the series of novels *The Roads to Freedom*.

Arendt, Hannah (1906–75), German-born American-Jewish political philosopher and social commentator, noted for her writings on totalitarianism and Jewish affairs. Arendt received wide acclaim for her book *Origins of Totalitarianism* (1951), and held appointments at the University of California at Berkeley, Princeton University and the University of Chicago. Among her many other writings are *The Human Condition* (1958), *Between Past and Future* (1961), *On Revolution* (1963) and the controversial *Eichmann in Jerusalem* (1963), based on her reports of the Nazi war trials.

Levinas, Emmanuel (1906–95), born to Lithuanian-Jewish parents but later naturalised French citizen. Levinas published the first full-length study of Husserl's work in French (in 1930), and as a co-translator of Husserl's *Cartesian Meditations* played an important role in introducing phenomenology into France. In his early work on Husserl the influence of Heidegger is already marked, and Levinas's methods and themes remain throughout deeply indebted to Heidegger's analysis of *Dasein* in *Being and Time*. However, he also asserts that his work is 'governed by a profound need to leave the climate of [Heidegger's] philosophy'. Of greatest significance in this movement away from Heidegger is Levinas's defence of the primacy of ethics (the relation to the other person) over ontology (the understanding of Being). His principle works include *Time and the Other* (1948; trans. 1987), *Totality and Infinity* (1961; trans. 1969) and *Otherwise than Being* (1974; trans. 1981).

Beauvoir, Simone de (1908–86), French philosopher and novelist and advocate of existentialism. In her first novel, *She Came to Stay* (1943; trans. 1949), de Beauvoir explored the existentialist dilemmas of individual freedom, action and responsibility. Later novels dealt with the same themes; among these are *The Blood of Others* (1944; trans., 1948) and *The Mandarins* (1954; trans. 1956), for which de Beauvoir received the Prix Goncourt. De Beauvoir is best known for her existentialist treatment of sexual difference in *The Second Sex* (1949; trans. 1953). The existentialist thesis that one is responsible for oneself is also advanced in her series of autobiographical works, notably *Memoirs of a Dutiful Daughter* (1958; trans. 1959) and *All Said and Done* (1972; trans. 1974). *Adieux: A Farewell to Sartre* (1984) is a memoir about her long-time colleague and partner Sartre.

Merleau-Ponty, Maurice (1908–61), French philosopher, whose existential phenomenology of the body opened a new field of philosophical investigation. His first important work was *The Structure of Behaviour* (1942; trans. 1963), a critique of behaviourism. His major work is *Phenomenology of Perception* (1945; trans. 1962) which tries to cut a path between the twin prejudices of empiricist-realism and intellectualist-idealism in the philosophy of perception. A number of essays on art, film, politics, psychology and religion have been collected in *Sense and Nonsense* (1948; trans. 1964). At the time of his death, he was working on a book, *The Visible and the Invisible* (1964; trans. 1968), in which he argues that the whole perceptual world has the sort of organic unity he had earlier attributed to the body and to works of art.

Lévi-Strauss, Claude Gustave (1908–), French anthropologist and leading proponent of the structuralist approach in social anthropology. He was interested in explaining why myths from different cultures from around the world seem so similar. He answers this question not by the content of myths, but by their structure. Like Rousseau he strongly challenged the idea of the supremacy of Western humanity. Among his books are *Elementary Structures of Kinship* (1949; trans. 1969), his autobiography, *Tristes Tropiques* (1955; trans. 1974), *The Savage Mind* (1962; 1966) and *The Raw and The Cooked* (1964; trans. 1969).

Camus, Albert (1913–60), French novelist and moralist, regarded as one of the finest philosophical writers of modern France. Camus's first published novel was, *The Outsider* (1942; trans. 1946). This work and the philosophical essay on which it is based, *The Myth of Sisyphus* (1942; trans. 1955), have clear connections with existentialist thought, although he had serious differences of opinion with Sartre. Of the plays that develop existentialist themes, *Caligula* (1944), produced in New York in 1960, is one of the best known.

Ricoeur, Paul (1913–2005), French philosopher. In his numerous writings on hermeneutics and phenomenology Ricoeur attempts to do justice to a call for textual objectivity and yet remain open to what texts may have to teach us about the construction of such objectivity. Ricoeur's hermeneutics represents his attempt to retain both science and art, while disallowing either an absolute status: 'Hermeneutics seems to me to be animated by this double motivation: willingness to suspect, willingness to listen'. Ricoeur has made significant contributions to debates in phenomenology, philosophy of language, philosophy of psychoanalysis, social theory and moral, political and legal philosophy. Among his best known writings are *Freud and Philosophy: An Essay on Interpretation* (1965; trans. 1970), *The Conflict of Interpretations: Essays in Hermeneutics* (1969; trans. 1974), *The Rule of Metaphor* (1975; trans. 1977) and *Time and Narrative* (3 volumes, 1983–85; trans. 1984–88).

Barthes, Roland (1915–80), French literary critic and social theorist. His book *On Racine* (1963; trans. 1976) was a landmark attempt to apply structuralist theory to literary works, claiming that the elements of such works are constituted in their relation to other textual elements. Today he is best known for his striking essays on and semiotic analyses of the codings that command our daily life in *Mythologies* (1957; trans. 1972). Some of his other works available in translation are *Elements of Semiology* (1965; trans. 1967), *S/Z* (1970; trans. 1974) and *The Pleasure of the Text* (1973; trans. 1976).

Althusser, Louis (1918–90), French political philosopher and leading structuralist Marxist theoretician. International attention came to Althusser with the publication in 1965 of *For Marx* (trans. 1969) closely followed, again in 1965, by *Reading Capital* (trans. 1970). His anti-empiricist and anti-humanist arguments set the terms of French philosophical debate during the 1970s and 80s. Of major significance is *Essays on Ideology* (1984) in which Althusser develops the idea that history is a 'process without a subject' meaning that social and economic structures have priority ('in the last instance') over individual human beings who are, in the process of socialisation, 'interpolated' *as* subjects.

Deleuze, Gilles (1925–95), French philosopher. Deleuze is widely credited with inaugurating the 'poststructuralist' movement with his 1962 book *Nietzsche and Philosophy* (trans. 1983), as well as providing its definitive text, the 1972 *Anti-Oedipus* (co-written with Félix Guattari; trans. 1977). The critical motif of production pervades his thought, and he defined his work in philosophy as 'the art of forming, inventing, and fabricating concepts' which attempt to give an account of (quasi-Kantian) transcendental conditions of the empirical realm in terms which are 'essentially pre-individual, non-personal and a-conceptual' – and non-transcendental. His other major works include *Difference and Repetition* (1968, trans. 1994) and *A Thousand Plateaus* (co-written with Félix Guattari, 1989; trans. 1987).

Lyotard, Jean-François (1925–98) French philosopher. Lyotard came to prominence with the publication of *The Postmodern Condition: A Report on Knowledge* (1979; trans. 1983), an explication of the idea of the postmodern and its relation to modernity. Along with the French social theorist Jean Baudrillard, Lyotard is often hailed (or condemned) as a 'high priest' of the postmodern world. His most important book, however, is *The Differend* (1983; trans. 1989), composed between 1973 and 1983, which investigates disputes where one of the interlocutors is divested of the means to argue. A case of a 'differend' between two parties takes place when the rules and regulation of the conflict that opposes them is done in the idiom of one of the parties, and where the wrong suffered by the other is not signified in that idiom.

Foucault, Michel (1926–84), French philosopher and historian. In *Madness and Civilization* (1961; trans. 1965), Foucault traced how, in the Western world, madness came to be thought of as mental illness. In *The Birth of the Clinic* (1963; trans. 1973) he analyses the emergence of the modern concept

. . .

of physical illness. In *The Order of Things* (1966; trans. 1970) he focuses on the different epistemic conventions that make up the historical a priori or 'episteme' of different historical periods. In *Discipline and Punish* (1975; trans. 1977) he investigates the way social power can come to constitutively order the lives of individuals by training their bodies, in much the same way that basic training may discipline and prepare a person to be a soldier. His last three books, *History of Sexuality, Volume I: An Introduction* (1976; trans. 1978), *The Use of Pleasure* (1984; trans. 1985) and *The Care of the Self* (1984; trans. 1986), are parts of an unfinished genealogy of sexuality.

Habermas, Jürgen (1929–), German social theorist and philosopher, widely known as the leading exponent of 'second generation' Critical Theory. Habermas's central claim – that human language and human communication in general already contain implicit intersubjective norms – is a development of Adorno's critique of traditional theory. However, for Habermas early Critical Theory conceded too much ground to the scepticism which it wished to contest, and he insists that universally valid norms governing communicative action can be isolated and stated. This is the project of his own *Theory of Communicative Action* (1981; trans. 1984). His other major works include *Toward a Rational Society* (1970; trans. 1971), *Knowledge and Human Interests* (1968; trans. 1971), *Legitimation Crisis* (1975; trans. 1976), *The Philosophical Discourse of Modernity* (1985; trans. 1987) and *Facts and Norms* (1992; trans. 1996).

Derrida, Jacques (1930–2004), French-Algerian philosopher, whose work introduced the idea of 'deconstruction' into contemporary thought and culture. Derrida's first published work was a long introduction to his own translation of Husserl's short essay *The Origin of Geometry* (1962; trans. 1978), but he burst onto the international scene in 1967 with the publication of *Speech and Phenomena* (trans. 1973), *Of Grammatology* (trans. 1977) and *Writing and Difference* (trans. 1978). Derrida's most famous claim is that the predicates traditionally thought to belong only to writing belong, in fact and in principle, to every species of sign whatsoever, including speech. Derrida's output was prodigious; some of his other major works include *Margins of Philosophy* (1972; trans. 1982), *The Truth in Painting* (1978; trans. 1987) *The Post Card* (1980; trans. 1987), *Of Spirit* (1987; trans. 1989), *The Other Heading* (1991; trans. 1992) and *Rogues* (2005).

Irigaray, Luce (1930–), Belgian-born philosopher, psychoanalyst and linguist. In the 1960s Irigaray trained as a psychoanalyst, attending Lacan's seminars, and her work remains indebted to Lacanian theory. Her second

. . .

successful doctoral thesis (the first was in linguistics) was published in
1974 as *Speculum of the Other Woman* (1974; trans. 1985) which includes
a major essay and critique of Freud's account of female sexuality and
subjectivity. In *Marine Lover of Friedrich Nietzsche* (1980; trans. 1991)
and *The Forgetting of Air in Heidegger* (1983; trans 1999), Irigaray
devotes her attention to Nietzsche and Heidegger respectively. The ambi-
guity in the title of her earlier book *This Sex Which Is Not One* (1977;
trans. 1985) nicely captures Irigaray's challenge to the dominant understanding of women's sexuality. Some of her most important other philosophical essays are collected in *An Ethics of Sexual Difference* (1984;
trans. 1993).

Kofman, Sarah (1934–94), French philosopher. Kofman wrote on a wide
range of philosophical figures, but it is Nietzsche who dominates her critical writings. Her books are only slowly becoming available in English, and
among her three books on Nietzsche only *Nietzsche and Metaphor* (1972;
trans. 1993) has been translated. The two books which placed her on the
feminist map are *The Enigma of Woman: Woman in Freud's Writings*
(1980; trans. 1985) and *Le respect des femmes (Kant et Rousseau)* (1982).
The latter raises the question of the applicability of Kant's categorical
imperative to women and argues that Rousseau's exhortations that women
conform to their nature have the effect of both normalising and naturalis-
ing women's subordination to men.

Badiou, Alain (1937–), Moroccan-born French philosopher, he is Emeritus
Professor of the Philosophy Department at the *Ecole Normale Supérieure*
and continues to teach a popular seminar at the *Collège International de
Philosophie* in Paris. Trained as a mathematician and also a published novelist, Badiou is one of the most original French philosophers today.
Influenced by Cantor as much as Plato, his work renews the understanding
of truth as the profound ally of processes of political emancipation and
transformation. His major publications include *Théorie du sujet* (1982),
L'Etre et l'Evénement (1988), *Deleuze: The Clamour of Being* (1997, trans.
2000), *Manifesto for Philosophy* (1989, trans. 1999) and *Ethics: An Essay
on the Understanding of Evil* (1993, trans. 2001).

Kristeva, Julia (1941–), Bulgarian-born French psychoanalyst and linguist.
Kristeva has written articles on poetic language, semiotics, psychoanalysis
and narrative. Her first collection of these, *Séméiotikè: Recherches Pour
une Sémanalyse*, was published in 1969, followed by *Le Texte du Roman*
(1970), and *La Révolution du Langage Poétique* (1974), in which she

. . .

explores the notion of subjectivity in language and history. Kristeva became a practising psychoanalyst in 1979, and has since written books and articles on a variety of topics and in various literary forms.

Le Dœuff, Michèle (1948–), French philosopher. Le Dœuff's work questions the boundaries of philosophy while insisting upon philosophy's importance. She is critical of professional philosophers' neglectful attitude to science, and argues that disputes within sciences are often philosophical. In her most well known book *Hipparchia's Choice* (1989; trans. 1991) she critically investigates philosophy's claim to achieve a pure clarity. In her view, philosophy is inevitably shaped by language, metaphor and power relations, including gender relations.

Žižek Slavoj (1949–), Slovenian philosopher and public intellectual. He is well known for his use of Lacanian ideas to develop new readings of popular culture. In addition to his work as an interpreter of Lacan and more recently Deleuze, he has written on numerous topics of general interest, such as fundamentalism, tolerance, political correctness, globalisation, human rights, myth, cyberspace, postmodernism, multiculturalism and Alfred Hitchcock. In 1990 he was a candidate for President of the Republic of Slovenia. His books include *The Sublime Object of Ideology* (1989), *The Ticklish Subject* (2000), *The Fragile Absolute* (2001) and *Organs Without Bodies: On Deleuze and Consequences* (2003).

Movements in the Stream

Among the many things that stand out in this list is the fact that not all the 'proper names' are professional philosophers. Philosophy is often considered the most richly interdisciplinary of all the humanities disciplines (the essential point here, in my view, is that it can be 'done' anywhere), but the serious interest in and affiliations with science, psychoanalysis, anthropology, history, politics and literature shown by a number of the thinkers on this list is striking. However, this is by no means true of all, and setting out the list of entries in a uniform manner might itself prove fairly misleading. In particular, what a listing format struggles to make perspicuous is the extent to which many of these authors are only 'more or less closely related' to each other, philosophically speaking.

One way around this formatting problem is to sort the usual suspects into smaller more or less separate clusters of coherence, more or less distinct streams or movements within the broad stream of philosophical thinking in the West. As we shall see, some of the standard groupings are more helpful and informative than others,[12] and the fact that the grouping 'analytic philosophy' is absent from this movements list certainly exacerbates the problems. Given the account I am proposing for what holds the Continental group together, however, it should be clear that I do not regard the absence of the analytic movement here as in any way a judgement call on my part. The absence of the analytic movement is not due to the fact that it differs, say, more sharply from these other movements than any of them do among themselves. On the contrary, the absence of the analytic movement from the list is, well, *analytic* since what is included is, precisely, the '*not-part*' part of analytic philosophy.[13] Nevertheless, the wide-angled view I presented in the last chapter reminds us that while there are numerous thematic and methodological convergences among the figures typically designated as 'the major Continental philosophers', there are also, and equally importantly, numerous thematic and methodological divergences and differences to be found too. There are a number of figures on the list who are, in fact, methodologically and thematically closer to many analytic philosophers than they are with many of the other figures on the Continental list. As one recent observer has noted 'Husserl has more in common with Frege than with Nietzsche, and Habermas more in common with Rawls than Marx'.[14]

And now bearing this in mind too I will present a list of the major movements and commonly identified groupings among 'the major Continental philosophers', again starting with Kant.

Kantianism. Central to Kant's critical philosophy is the distinction between things considered as they are 'in themselves' and things conceived in so far as we are conscious of them, 'appearances'. Kant claims that we can know nothing whatsoever about things in themselves, but only as they appear to us. Appearances (empirically real things) are understood as structured by the ways in which we must represent and think about them, conditions ultimately grounded in the conditions of unity of the self-conscious subject itself (the 'unity of apperception').

Major representative: Kant.

German Idealism. Kant's immediate followers were dissatisfied with two aspects of his idealism. The first is the notion of the thing in itself. The

. . .

---

second is the lack of systematicity. The former was regarded as a dogmatic remnant from transcendental realism. The latter concerns the fact that Kant does not begin from a self-evident first principle and derive everything from this. It is true that Kant arrived at an ultimate condition of knowledge in the unity of apperception, but what was required by his followers was that philosophy begin with something like this principle. Otherwise concepts and distinctions will be introduced before they have been accounted for.

Major representatives: Fichte, Schelling, Hegel.

Hermeneutics. For hermeneutists we always bring certain presuppositions or 'prejudices' to a reading of a text, to a dialogue or argument with another, or to an experience. While some of these count as prejudices in the pejorative sense and may be eliminable, in general they are regarded as presuppositions which make knowledge and understanding possible and are not only a negative limitation. It is only from the perspective of projecting a God's eye view that the necessity of such 'prejudices' counts as a failing or a lack. The inevitability of prejudices in every investigation, including an investigation of prejudices, gives rise to the dynamic (non-vicious) 'hermeneutic circle' where, in understanding and interpretation, part and whole are related in a circular way: in order to understand the whole it is necessary to understand the parts and vice versa, and as one's understanding of a part develops or changes this will 'feed back' into one's grasp of the whole.

Major representatives: Schleiermacher, Dilthey, Heidegger, Gadamer, Ricoeur.

Philosophy of life. What unites these authors is their concern to rearticulate the account of the relation between human beings and the world they inhabit in order to show the limits of theoretical reason, and to undermine the picture of mental life as primarily cognitive, rational and conceptual. Philosophers of life place great stress on concrete and organic processes, which is allied to the idea that life is not to be grasped by theoretical systematicity, as supposed by the German idealists. This does not mean that such thinkers give up all attempts at being systematic but that the unity they seek is a 'concrete whole' (e.g. 'my life'), not a theoretical construction (e.g. 'a rational mind').

Major representatives: Schopenhauer, Nietzsche, Bergson.

Young Hegelians. Following Hegel's death in 1831 two antithetical Hegelian schools developed: the so-called 'Old' Hegelians and the 'Young' Hegelians, later also categorised as 'Right' and 'Left' Hegelians. Both groups

. . .

agreed with Hegel that 'what is rational is actual and what is actual is rational', but they differed over its significance. In the view of the Young Hegelians it might be the case, in principle, that the actual is rational, but in fact it most assuredly is not. Nevertheless, they were alike convinced in a 'second creation' to come; that is, an unquestioned eschatological belief that a new order was immanent defines the outlook (and for some the appeal) of the Young Hegelians. The group found its first leader in Ludwig Feuerbach.

Major representatives: Feuerbach and Marx, but also Bruno Bauer, Edgar Bauer, Moses Hess, Karl Schmidt, Arnold Ruge, Max Stirner.

Philosophy of existence. Like philosophers of life, philosophers of existence or 'existentialists' advocate an understanding of what is concrete and particular rather than what is abstract and universal. If philosophy is understood as the systematic study of universal and general truths, then philosophy of existence is the anti-philosophical movement *par excellence*. One of the most influential practitioners of suspicion about systematic philosophy was Kierkegaard in his resistance to Hegel's efforts at absolute thought. Kierkegaard accuses Hegel of building a great mansion without doors, in which the human being is left to live in the outhouse. It is in the realisation of the way in which existence is situated beyond the reach of systematic and formal logical impositions that a wide range of existential critiques of philosophy have been advanced. The lived reality of 'being in the world' is usually what philosophers of existence mean by 'existence'. Since Sartre (who claimed to be following Heidegger) the idea that human beings are fundamentally self-creative (or that, for human beings, 'existence precedes essence') has become a common slogan of existentialist philosophy.

Major representatives: Kierkegaard, Nietzsche, Buber, Jaspers, Marcel, Heidegger, Sartre, Merleau-Ponty, de Beauvoir, Camus.

Phenomenology. Kant's influence on phenomenology is pervasive. Although Kant did not make use of the term in his main works, his emphasis on the unifying and structuring function of consciousness, as exemplified by the unity of apperception, set the stage for Brentano's discussion of the intentionality of consciousness, and Kant's ongoing concern about the relation between the phenomenal and noumenal realms provides a crucial point of departure for many subsequent phenomenological discussions of 'the Being of the phenomenon'. While phenomenology is a historical movement with various more or less continuous themes, both Husserl and

. . .

Heidegger preferred to explain the title by tracing its etymology to its Greek roots, in which it signified, as Heidegger put it, 'to let that which shows itself be seen from itself in the very way in which it shows itself from itself'. One can see why Heidegger called the idea of 'descriptive phenomenology' a tautology, but it is important to note that for Husserl and Heidegger the 'phenomena' of phenomenology are not phenomena in the ordinary sense (things, beings). Heidegger explicitly recalls the Kantian notion of forms of sensible intuition when he notes that his concern as a phenomenologist is not with those phenomena encountered within experience but with what makes any such encounter possible. The phenomenon of phenomenology is thus 'that which already shows itself in the appearance as prior to the 'phenomenon' as ordinarily understood'.

Major representatives: Brentano, Husserl, Jaspers, Heidegger, Gadamer, Sartre, Levinas, Arendt, de Beauvoir, Merleau-Ponty.

Marxist political philosophy. A central tenet of Marxist philosophy is that the ways in which many social divisions express themselves (e.g. gender and racial divisions) are dependent on the differing historico-economic and economic-class circumstances in which they occur. Some have found this to be an overly reductive conception of social reality, others suggest that to grasp such divisions within economic contexts is not to undervalue them. Nevertheless, the history of Marxism in Europe is a history of attempts to either create a synthesis of Marx with other thinkers or to deepen the understanding of the social and ideological 'infrastructure' in order to overcome its apparent economism. Georg Lukács's interpretation of Marx's notion of alienation owes much to Weber's idea of the increasing rationalisation of society. The Italian communist Antonio Gramsci stressed the role of ideology in civil society in the construction of political hegemony. The appeal of Marxism is that it gives powerful intellectual backing to irreducibly normative responses to the iniquities of the modern capitalist world, and thus gives grounds to the hope that a system which ought to disintegrate will eventually do so.

Major representatives: Marx, Lukács, Gramsci, and also Friedrich Engels, the Frankfurt School, later Sartre, Althusser.

Neo-Kantianism. While phenomenology developed the ontological implications of Kantianism, with Heidegger in particular insisting that Kant's goal was a conceptual clarification of our a priori grasp of 'what it is to be an object' (understanding of Being), the neo-Kantians stressed the epistemological implications, seeking in the First Critique a 'theory of
. . .

knowledge' and a philosophy of science. The connections to phenomenology are, however, much greater than is often acknowledged. Cassirer, for example, claims to provide a phenomenology that centres on the power of human symbolisation. It is, he argues, our ability to symbolise our experience that has led to the flowering of human culture, whether in art or in science. Many of the neo-Kantians were concerned to give an account of the distinction between the natural and the human sciences, typically through transcendental analyses of the constitution of all 'objects' of human concern whether scientific, aesthetic or moral.

Major representatives: Hermann Cohen, Heinrich Rickert, Ernst Cassirer, Nicolai Hartmann and also Paul Natorp.

Freudian psychoanalytic theory. A central theme in Freud's understanding of human psychology is the theory of wish-fulfilment. In many cases, he claimed, a desire is pacified not through a real action which satisfies it (e.g. the desire for a drink of water being pacified by drinking water) but a kind of short-circuiting of this route in which the mind produces a pacifying representation of satisfaction for itself (e.g. the desire for a drink of water being pacified for someone who is asleep by her dreaming that she is drinking water). Moreover, in Freud's view the goal of many of our most constant and basic desires is not realistic satisfaction but representational pacification. Such desires are typically expressed in a symbolic or metaphorical form, a feature of Freud's account which was to be developed by the French psychoanalyst Jacques Lacan.

Major representatives: Sigmund Freud, Jacques Lacan, but also a significant influence on the Frankfurt School and Critical Theory.

Structuralism. 'What is structuralism?' Roland Barthes asked in 1963: 'Not a school, not even a movement (at least not yet), for most of the authors ordinarily labelled with this word are unaware of being united by any solidarity of doctrine or commitment. Nor is it a vocabulary'. Nevertheless, there is a unifying vision that connects the various authors convinced by the work of Saussure in linguistics: namely, that the fundamental features of human life – those to be found in language, but also in kinship and society, in literature and in psychology – are relational and structural rather than intrinsic or substantial. That is, they cannot be discovered by looking at factual elements given to observation and perception but only by looking beyond these to the relations and structures that constitute them. These structures may be hidden from view, but the phenomena that are open to view emanate or flow from these hidden forms. The concern to explore

. . .

networks of relationships that unite and form structures thus gives analytical priority to wholes and totalities rather than particular individuals and concrete events.

Major representatives: Saussure, Lacan, Lévi-Strauss, Barthes, Althusser.

Frankfurt School and Critical theory. Critical theorists have attempted to develop interdisciplinary collaboration between philosophy and the human sciences in ways which question the nature and limits of the division of intellectual labour which has so powerfully determined their relationship in the modern era. Critical theorists do not share substantive social, historical or conceptual theses, nor a common method. What unifies them, however, can be gleaned in their shared title: their commitment to theoretical work which is 'critical' – in contrast to traditional 'descriptive' theories which claim to be able to separate fact and value – and to develop criticisms that are 'theoretical' – in contrast to sociological relativism which supposes that truth claims are simply decided by whether or not they serve the right social interest. The Institute for Social Research was opened in Frankfurt by Felix Weil, the Marxist son of a grain millionaire, in 1924. The Institute initially had strong ties to the Soviet socialist model and aimed to advance the study of Marxism in Germany. Following the appointment of Horkheimer to the directorship in 1930 its leading members were almost uniformly critical of the Soviet Union, while remaining deeply attached to Marx's own work.

Of those who are typically given the title of major representative in this grouping, some bear it fairly – Horkheimer, Adorno, Habermas – others rather less fairly – Bloch, Benjamin, Marcuse.

Lacanian theory. A central feature of Lacan's inheritance of Freudian theory is the effort to expose psychoanalytic discourse to theoretical developments within the human sciences, in particular to merge psychoanalysis with philosophy, linguistics and anthropology. His seminars and papers contain complex references to Hegel, Heidegger and Lévi-Strauss as well as (more famously) Saussure. Central to Lacan's account of our lives as individual 'subjects' is his view of our entry into language, which is taken to have three interdependent and interpenetrating 'registers': the symbolic, the imaginary and the real. The symbolic order is the order of signs 'bound together by specific laws' (the prohibition of incest is a socio-symbolic law for Lacan). The imaginary realm is the field wherein ideas (or, more precisely, illusions) of individuality are maintained. And the real, not to be confused with standard conceptions of reality, is what is not representable in

. . .

discourse at all: it is a dimension of existence behind and beyond anything that can be grasped by signs and symbols, and is resistant to symbolisation. Irigaray has argued that the dominance of the symbolic order by signs of masculinity and the father figure means that the experience of the specifically feminine subject is generated through her relation to the real rather than the symbolic order.

Major representatives: Lacan, Irigaray, Žižek.

Poststructuralism. This contemporary grouping has a real chance of being thought of as made up of 'Continental philosophers' in a sense other than the merely negative one of 'not being analytic philosophers'. For it is a feature of their work that, unlike most contemporary analytic philosophers, they have affinities with, relationships to and sometimes a serious working interest in a great number of the authors cited as the usual suspects. And this is so despite the fact that they do not themselves belong to the movements that are usually associated with those authors. However, they differ among themselves enormously and the impression of homogeneity created by the title is fundamentally misleading. The thinkers included in this group are distinctively eclectic. They have debts all over the place, including for some debts to analytic philosophy. The so-called 'poststructuralists' are predominantly contemporary French philosophers, and their work is sometimes more or as much 'post'-Kantian, 'post'-phenomenological, 'post'-existentialist, 'post'-Marxist or 'post'-Freudian, as it is 'post'-structuralist. It is because of the dominance of structuralist themes in French philosophy in the 1960s and 1970s, and the reaction against that dominance by a new generation of French thinkers, that gave rise to the current title in the Anglo-American reception of their work. A more accurate title might have been 'recent French philosophy' except for the fact that soon enough it won't be recent and many thinkers who are of significance to this generation are not French: Paul de Man, Hillis Miller, Judith Butler and, in general, the leading 'Continental philosophers' in Britain and America are part of this loose network of thinkers who are hard to place except in the sense they have affinities with, relationships to and a serious working interest in a great number of the authors cited as the usual suspects.

Major representatives: Deleuze, Foucault, Lyotard, Derrida, French feminism (see below), Badiou.

French feminism. This title, like the previous one, is a peculiar invention. In fact it is a kind of microcosm for 'Continental philosophy' as a whole,

. . .

except that its originators were more well-meaning. Created by an Anglo-American readership, the title oversimplifies by creating the misleading impression of homogeneity between diverse (although exclusively female) thinkers who live in France. Le Dœuff, for example, finds little to praise in Irigaray's work. One commentator notes that these days 'the indignity and deceptiveness of this sort of homogenization is widely recognized'.[15] This is spot on and precisely what I would like to see more widely recognized about the collection of the usual suspects of 'Continental philosophy' as a whole.

Major representatives: Irigaray, Kofman, Kristeva, Le Dœuff.

There we have it then, the usual suspects and their commonly acknowledged groupings. I am sure I could have done a better job in giving thumbnail sketches of the listed thinkers. And I am sure no reader of the lists will seriously regard them as providing any kind of substitute for a reading of the work listed in them. In any case that was not my purpose in providing them. Of course, it helps newcomers to see it all held together in one place and in a form that gives some kind of 'at a glance' sense of the waters. However, unless the lists of the usual suspects and their commonly acknowledged groupings are appreciated in their internal diversity, what is given-at-a-glance here will still, in view of the (necessary) absence of the analytic movement, be seriously misleading. In the next two chapters I will attempt more systematically to dismantle the reasons that have sustained the idea that an introduction to these authors might provide an introduction to a distinctive philosophical tradition.

However, before I do, and to bring this 'at a glance' phase of the discussion to a close, it will prove helpful finally to draw a 'map' that integrates the preceding descriptions by using the list of movements in the stream to make groupings among the list of the usual suspects. The rough map in Figure 3.1 below is formed by accurately listing the usual suspects by date of birth on the vertical axis and in an arbitrary but hopefully schematically helpful distribution along the horizontal axis. The result of completing the map's contours (which I invite you to do if you own this book) does nothing to support the idea of a Continental tradition. But, of course, that is just fine by me.

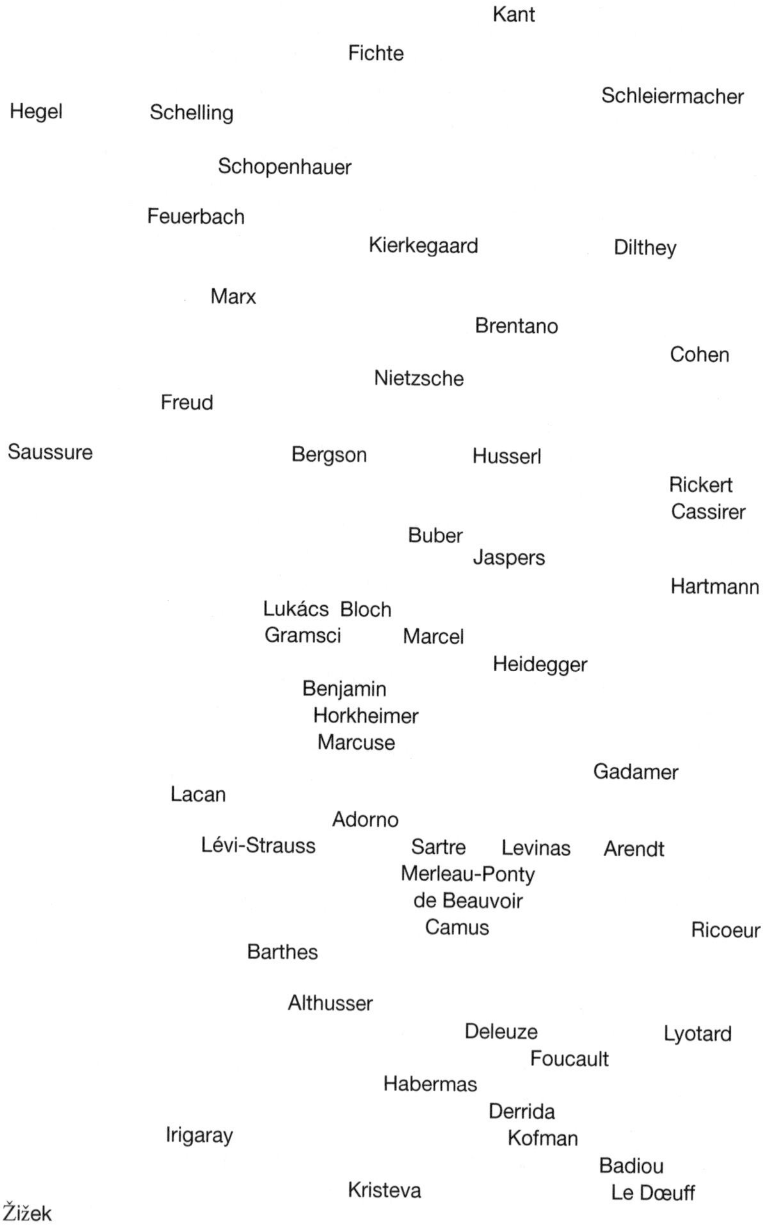

Kant

Fichte

Schleiermacher

Hegel   Schelling

Schopenhauer

Feuerbach

Kierkegaard   Dilthey

Marx

Brentano

Cohen

Nietzsche

Freud

Saussure   Bergson   Husserl

Rickert
Cassirer

Buber

Jaspers

Hartmann

Lukács Bloch
Gramsci   Marcel

Heidegger

Benjamin
Horkheimer
Marcuse

Gadamer

Lacan

Adorno

Lévi-Strauss   Sartre   Levinas   Arendt
Merleau-Ponty
de Beauvoir
Camus   Ricoeur

Barthes

Althusser

Deleuze   Lyotard
Foucault

Habermas

Derrida

Irigaray   Kofman

Badiou
Kristeva   Le Dœuff

Žižek

Figure 3.1 *A map of Continental philosophy.*

Notes

1. The kind of resources typically available to analytic philosophers are framed by the distinctions I sketched at the end of the last chapter, distinctions that define Continental philosophy as the Other or *'not part'* part of analytic philosophy.
2. Jacques Derrida, *The Post Card*, Chicago: University of Chicago Press, 1987, p. 4.
3. Why do people who find Derrida so awful invent such awful names to (mis)represent what he is doing? Words like 'deconstructivist' or 'deconstructivism' or 'deconstructionism' are mentioned as if they were citing something (as if at arm's length like avoiding a bad smell) but it is their own autistic invention.
4. The second presupposes the first not in the sense that one must first go through the first response, but in the sense that the first is (as it were) *swallowed down* by anyone who makes the second.
5. Simon Critchley, 'Introduction', in *A Companion to Continental Philosophy*, eds S. Critchley and W. Schroeder, Oxford: Blackwell, 1998, p. 5.
6. Bernard Williams, 'Contemporary Philosophy: A Second Look', in *The Blackwell Companion to Philosophy*, eds N. Bunnin and E. P. Tsui-James, Oxford: Blackwell, 1996, p. 27.
7. The joke is made (in print) by Richard Rorty in *Contingency, Irony and Solidarity*, Cambridge: CUP, 1989, p. 81. The idea is that one way of delineating analytic from Continental philosophy is that the former is primarily concerned with philosophical problems (the nature of meaning, the problem of intersubjectivity, the intentionality of consciousness, etc.) while the latter simply discusses what other people have written.
8. See Simon Critchley, 'Introduction', p. 2.
9. Simon Critchley, 'Introduction', p. 9.
10. Originally – but *entirely*? Kant is a clear exception. Indeed, it is in a differential response to Kant that some would see 'the parting of the ways'. I will deal with that idea in Chapter 5.
11. In constructing these entries I have made extensive use of the survey essays in *The Edinburgh Encyclopedia of Continental Philosophy*, ed. S. Glendinning. There is one group of thinkers included in that encyclopedia who I have omitted from this list despite the fact that they belong to it for both historical and methodological reasons: namely, the British idealists of the late nineteenth century. I will bring them into the picture in the next chapter, but along with A. N. Whitehead (whose later, post-logicist, process philosophy also deserves a special mention) I am leaving them out of this (also) geographically Continental collection.
12. On this point I would ask that readers who are just skimming the entries on these movements in the stream pay particular attention to the observations made in the final two groupings.
13. It should be remembered that this movement (which is, as I am trying to show, of peculiar significance for the grouping 'Continental philosophy'

as such) is, from a wide-angled view, one movement among others in the stream of Western thought a great swathe of which is included here.

14. From Brian Leiter's, 'Note on analytic and Continental philosophy' in his 'Gourmet Report' which had been published for some time (but alas no more) by Blackwell at http://www.blackwellpublishers.co.uk/gourmet for 2001. Leiter's more recent reports have backtracked somewhat on the unhelpfulness of the distinction between analytic and Continental philosophy.

15. Stella Sandford, 'Johnny Foreigner', *Radical Philosophy*, no. 102, 2000, p. 45.

4

The Analytic Perspective on the Idea

Ryle and the Gulf-Seekers

The trajectory of this book is entering its most crucial phase. I have promised to look at the major reasons and arguments (perhaps I should say more neutrally that I will look at 'major texts') presented by analytic philosophers who have affirmed or embraced the idea of what Gilbert Ryle called the 'wide gulf' between Anglo-Saxon 'philosophical analysis' and philosophy on 'the Continent'.[1] It is now time to do so. The texts I will look at are all from the same period: the late 1950s.[2] As we shall see, the idea of the gulf was already well established by then, but it was not so confidently or openly expressed before then. The basic point, however, is that the understanding of the idea of Continental philosophy articulated in these texts is the one which is, more or less, still with us today.[3]

The situation we are dealing with is one where communication has all but broken down between self-styled analytic philosophers and other voices in the contemporary philosophical culture. My major interpretive proposal about this is to suggest that the thinking about the breakdown that is an appeal to the idea of a division between analytic and Continental philosophy does not so much as capture the rotten scene as it is part of it. My ultimate aim in this book is to help us to resist this mess and encourage a greater clarity in our thinking and greater refinement in our inhabitation of our philosophical culture. And my basic strategy in this regard is to show how very questionable is the very idea of a distinctive Continental tradition. In this chapter I will engage with this theme by exploring texts that belong centrally to the rotten scene we are still largely faced with, texts which have strongly affirmed the idea of (and so cultivated the reality of) a gulf-stricken culture. In doing so I hope to make it clear why it came about that Continental philosophy became the analytic tag for what must be excluded from a healthy philosophical culture.

We can find something like a *locus classicus* for the terms and tone of analytic philosophy's (self-)developing conception of the division in the contemporary philosophical culture in Gilbert Ryle's address to a conference entitled 'La Philosophie Analytique' held at Royaumont, north of Paris, in 1958. The conference had been organised by French-speaking philosophers who, while clearly not unfamiliar with the published work of their Anglophone contemporaries, sought discussion with, among others, thinkers from the already notoriously insular 'Oxford School' of philosophical analysis. While the French title of the conference nicely anticipates the current distinction between analytic and Continental philosophy, these terms had yet to become the everyday currency of English-language metaphilosophy. The dominant vocabulary was, in fact, geographical and national, and for Ryle and his fellow Oxford analysts, Continental philosophy still meant, basically, 'philosophical work on the European Continent'.

Nevertheless, the familiar (evaluative) contrast was definitely being prepared for. The very title of Ryle's contribution, 'Phenomenology versus *The Concept of Mind*', reflected and encouraged the British contingent's assumption of, and perhaps desire for, confrontation, conflict, opposition and division. And some of the contents of Ryle's talk (mis)treated the participants to some of the most extraordinary and inflammatory remarks ever (publicly) voiced on the superiority of 'Anglo-Saxon' or 'English-speaking' philosophy over its 'Continental' rival.

Ryle began with what appeared to be a brief summary of Husserl's phenomenology. The sentence which concludes that summary, however, gave it an unexpected but important spin: 'This caricature of Husserl's phenomenology is intended to show up by contrast some of the predominant features of recent philosophy and in particular of the philosophy of mind in the English-speaking world'.[4] In this sentence we see the signals of two of the most abiding features of standard presentations of analytic philosophy: first, that it is drawn through a contrast to some other style of philosophy; and second, and more seriously, that this other is presented without the kind of critical care which analytic philosophers would (quite rightly) expect if someone were presenting *their* work. Ryle's case is developed by contrast not with Husserl's philosophy (although he sometimes puts it that way and some of his arguments against Husserl's conception of knowledge seem to me sound, and as Ryle more or less admits soundly phenomenological) but with a caricature of Husserl's philosophy. Ryle seems to have been happily unconcerned by the threat this posed to his analysis. When in discussion he was politely reproached by the founder of the Husserl archives in Louvain, Herman van Breda, for 'not having sufficiently read his Husserl',[5] Ryle bluntly declared that he 'care[d] little' whether the caricature resembled Husserl and hoped that the debate would not 'degenerate' into a 'colloquium on Husserl'.[6]

Apparently content with caricature then, Ryle's address makes use of it to 'show up' by contrast the distinctive Anglo-Saxon alternative. Of course, the trouble now is that we cannot be confident that this represents a genuine contrast to a bad philosophical road that was actually being followed. Still, Ryle's two basic claims are worth quoting in full, if only to acquaint newcomers with the mode of Ryle's philosophical gulf-seeking:

1. Apart from one or two brief flirtations, British thinkers have showed no inclination to assimilate philosophical to scientific inquiries; and a fortiori no inclination to puff philosophy up into the Science of sciences. Conceptual inquiries differ from scientific inquiries not in hierarchical rank but in type. They are not higher or lower, since they are not on the same ladder. I guess that our thinkers have been immunised against the idea of philosophy as the Mistress Science by the fact that their daily lives in Cambridge and Oxford Colleges have kept them in personal contact with real scientists. Claims to Führership vanish when postprandial joking begins. Husserl wrote as if he had never met a scientist – or a joke.

2. Even inside philosophy, no privileged position has with us been accorded to the philosophy of mind. Certainly, with us as elsewhere, and in this century as in other centuries, many philosophers have been primarily interested in problems of epistemology, of ethics, of politics, and of jurisprudence. But many others have been primarily interested in the philosophy of mathematics, of physics, and of biology. We have not worried our heads over the question Which philosopher ought to be Führer? If we did ask ourselves this question, we should mostly be inclined to say that it is logical theory that does or should control other conceptual inquiries, though even this control would be advisory rather than dictatorial. At least the main lines of our philosophical thinking during this century can be fully understood only by someone who has studied the massive developments of our logical theory. This fact is partly responsible for the wide gulf that has existed for three-quarters of a century between Anglo-Saxon and Continental philosophy. For, on

the Continent during this century, logical studies have, unfortunately, been left unfathered by most philosophy departments and cared for, if at all, only in a few departments of mathematics.[7]

Now all of that is, because outrageous, arrogant and complacent, crazily funny. But, what would Ryle, 'King' if not 'Führer' of British philosophy at the time,[8] have thought had his own work, or, say, that of G. E. Moore or Bertrand Russell, been mistreated in this way. Enjoy the joke?

Joke or no joke, the use of caricature is bad all round. At a time when memories of the Second World War were still vivid, Ryles chides (Jewish born) Husserl for claiming Führership for philosophy. But in discussion afterwards he shows no interest in the point from the audience that many philosophers, including Aristotle and Kant, had 'defended a certain priority for philosophy', and he (Ryle) would not 'consider ridiculing *them*'.[9] Biographer of both Russell and Wittgenstein, Ray Monk raises a further complaint against the viability of a national distinction to underwrite Ryle's reference to 'the massive developments' of '*our* logical theory':

> *Our* logical theory? But didn't Russell learn his logic from an Italian (Peano), and a whole lot of Germans (Cantor, Weierstrass, Dedekind and Frege)? In the following section of Ryle's paper, it transpires that what he means by 'the massive developments of our logical theory' is the progression from Russell's theory of descriptions to Wittgenstein's theories of meaning in, first, *Tractatus Logico-Philosophicus* and then *Philosophical Investigations*. These developments he characterizes as 'The *Cambridge* Transformation of the Theory of Concepts', thus bypassing the slightly awkward fact that Wittgenstein was more Germanic than Anglo-Saxon. Wittgenstein, for all that he wrote in German and felt like an alien in England, was, it seems, a Cambridge man through and through, and not really a 'Continental' at all.[10]

Ryle, however, prefers to be blind to the extent to which his intellectual world has Continental debts and is determined to affirm what he calls a 'wide gulf' between 'Anglo-Saxon and Continental philosophy'. Yet, and this is crucial, it is not simply the terms of Ryle's distinction which are inadequate or distorting.[11] One of the participants at the conference was Maurice Merleau-Ponty, a major French phenomenologist and an indebted reader of Husserl. In discussion he raised a series of points seeking clarification from Ryle. The points were varied, but they were posed not to exhibit differences or show up contrasts but in order to 'make precise how far our agreement goes'. For, like other participants, he was not convinced by Ryle's talk of a philosophical 'gulf' or of a major rift in the European philosophical culture: 'I have also had the impression, while listening to Mr Ryle, that what he was saying was not so strange to us, and that the distance, if there is a distance, is one that he puts between us rather than one I find there.'[12]

For reasons I will return to, L. J. Cohen later described the conference at Royaumont as 'the sort of set piece affair . . . where the participants meet once, as it were, and rather sterilely agree to differ'.[13] The truth seems rather more to be that the Oxford analysts had *already decided* that communication was or should be impossible. They were only too happy it seems to give the impression that attempts to 'make precise how far our agreement goes' were worthless. So successful were they in that regard, so strong was this impression, that memories of the event have been affected by it. Relying on recollections from someone who had attended the event nearly forty years ago, Simon Critchley reports that Ryle rudely closed off the opportunity for communication by dismissing a suggestion from Merleau-Ponty that their 'programme is the same' with a blunt '*I hope not*'.[14]

Ryle was rude, but not quite that rude. And as we have just seen Merleau-Ponty's offer of an olive branch regarding 'the distance between us' was not so simplistic either. As the transcript of the conference indicates the recollection is mistaken. What Ryle actually said was that if he were asked whether his position was 'strictly in agreement' with 'the programme outlined at the beginning of the century by Russell and refined by Wittgenstein and some others' he would say: '*I certainly hope not*'.[15] It was a distance *within* the analytic movement that he was insisting on at that point, not a distance between that movement and phenomenology. But note a nuance in Ryle's remarks. Affirming a distance from Russell and Wittgenstein was not, Ryle pointedly insisted, intended 'to say anything disagreeable about Russell, Wittgenstein or anyone else' but only to affirm the value of independent thinking. And he happily accepted that Russell and Wittgenstein 'opened some pathways' to which he owed a great deal. The idea of a distance between the analytic movement and the phenomenological movement on the Continent is not mentioned at that point, but it was, of course, the topic of the whole paper. And it seems to me indisputable that Ryle's paper taken as a whole was very precisely intended to say something 'disagreeable' about phenomenology on the Continent. So even if he did not say what Critchley's source reports him as saying, in everything that he said he certainly wanted to make things look that way. As noted already, the fact that the title of Ryle's paper says phenomenology 'versus' *The Concept of Mind* serves only to accentuate the intent to find distance. On the other hand, what it invites us massively to downplay is a quietly acknowledged point that could have been a point of departure for a discussion which, had Ryle wanted it to, could have opened rather than closed off certain pathways: namely, that *The Concept of Mind* can itself be fairly understood as a 'sustained essay in phenomenology'.[16]

Hare on Schooling Philosophers

The putative impossibility of international philosophical communication was also the theme of another early gulf-seeking text: R. M. Hare's lecture on British philosophy 'given at a number of German centres in the summer of 1957'.[17] In his lecture, Hare explores what he calls the 'two different ways' in which philosophy is currently studied, ways concerning which 'one might be forgiven for thinking . . . are really two quite different subjects'.[18] Like Ryle's, Hare's metaphilosophical lexicon is national, and the 'two different ways' are named as British and German philosophy. Again like Ryle, Hare performs the finesse of identifying British philosophy with work being done at 'the older British universities' and especially Oxford. German philosophy, on the other hand, is not explicitly identified with anything at all. And as we shall see, Hare is even more willing than Ryle to make use of and recourse to caricature.

Hare's initial remarks, however, comprise a fragrant homily to the Oxford tutorial system. In such a system, Hare insists, a student of philosophy will be taught 'how to think more clearly and to the point', taught, that is, 'to express his thought clearly to himself and to others; to make distinctions where there are distinctions to be made, and thus avoid unnecessary confusion – and not to use long words (or short ones) without being able to explain what they mean'.[19]

Hare's discussion of twentieth-century Oxford teaching practices is, however, introduced so as to flag up the basic characteristics of contemporary Oxford (and by implication British) philosophy generally. That is, what he calls British philosophy is presented as guided by the intellectual virtues it teaches, viz. 'clarity, relevance and brevity'.[20] Such virtues will then ensure that arguments between 'British philosophers' can circulate and develop through the defence and refutation of work with 'an unambiguously stated thesis'.[21] This, according to Hare, is the central characteristic and great strength of British philosophical analysis.

The unambiguously stated thesis of Hare's paper is that British and German philosophy is 'the same subject studied in two different ways'. The unstated, less clear, but certainly no less unambiguous thesis is that the German philosophical way is the *wrong* philosophical way. Supposing, as is in fact constantly invited, the contrast to the British way is, even when unstated as such, the German way, then the latter enjoys the 'delights of erecting, in solitary thought, imposing edifices – of writing huge volumes which only a handful of people will ever understand';[22] and the typical author of such 'long or difficult books'[23] or 'monstrous philosophical edifices'[24] likes to 'collect a private coterie to listen to him';[25] and he will not be averse to 'the turning of philosophy into *mystique*'[26] or to producing 'verbiage' disguised as 'serious metaphysical inquiry'.[27] In short, according to Hare, 'German philosophy' thrives on and finds 'uplifting' work characterised by 'ambiguities and evasions and rhetoric', i.e. just those characteristics which 'British philosophers' regard 'as the mark of a philosopher who has not learnt his craft'.[28]

A grave nod. And yet who are the 'German philosophers' who have so despoiled the virtues of the subject called philosophy? A little later Hare expresses special annoyance at 'German philosophers' who 'have chosen to ignore [the] important developments made by Vienna Circle positivism' and who 'carry on in their old ways as if nothing had happened'.[29] But no names and no examples are given.

Hare may not name names here, but the impatience shown towards philosophical writings that retain a certain patience towards questions that positivism sought to foreclose seems to have a pointed relevance to the opening of Heidegger's (yes, long and difficult book) *Being and Time* and its openness to what he (Heidegger) calls 'the question of Being'.[30] Of course, Heidegger knows very well that his question will not be well received – 'if anyone continues to ask it he is charged with an error of method'[31] – but even so he still looks like a prime candidate for Hare's annoyance. It would seem that Hare's impatience with a willingness to pursue such (in Hare's philosophical eyes) 'metaphysical' questions has just the kind of methodological ground that Heidegger anticipates. For Hare, philosophers who 'carry on in their old ways' are not just taking an alternative philosophical path but overlooking what today we have come to recognise as the methodological primacy of the *logically prior* question of whether their 'statements' on such 'meta-physical' topics actually 'mean something'.[32] And, naturally, if their 'statements' do not mean something then they should just stop advancing them as if they do; and if they do mean something, well this meaning should be clearly explained and not left in a dark and enigmatic obscurity. On this view, the best one can say is that a philosopher who, in our times, carries on with such 'metaphysical' matters 'as if nothing had happened' shows a seriously annoying willingness to use words whose meaning is (at least) not clear.

In Hare's view, then, if Heidegger (or other such German philosophers) manages to get a following (if, in Hare's words, he manages to 'collect a private coterie to listen to him') this will most likely be achieved through a kind of linguistic sleight of hand: producing an impression of 'serious metaphysical inquiry' by means of impressive sounding 'verbiage' marked by 'ambiguities and evasions and rhetoric'. Such a philosopher trades on making use of words he has not clearly defined and which, logically speaking, even he himself cannot understand. The fact that Heidegger anticipates that others will come who will charge him with 'an error of method' doesn't mean he hasn't made one.

Yet it seems to me significant that had Hare cared to read even the first few pages of the opening sections of *Being and Time* (or if he did find time to read them, then to re-read them with a little more care), it might have dawned on him that the question of the meaning of the words we use, and of our understanding or non-understanding of them, is absolutely central to Heidegger's discussion too. It is surely striking (and unmissable I would think) that Heidegger right from the start identifies his interest in the question of Being as bound up with a kind of empuzzlement regarding what we *mean* and *understand* by the expression 'Being'.[33] The question Heidegger wishes to 'raise anew' is precisely *'the question of the meaning* [Sinn] *of Being'*.[34] He is interested, therefore, in *what is understood* in 'any understanding of Being whatsoever'.[35]

So Heidegger is concerned straight away with issues of meaning and understanding. Nevertheless, one might still balk at the assumption that there *is* some 'what' that is the 'what is understood' in the particular case Heidegger is concerned with. What justification is there for thinking that one has asked a good question here? May it not be that the question itself simply has no meaning at all and is pure nonsense? That it is a 'good question' is, I think, precisely what is *wagered* by

Heidegger in *Being and Time*. Whether one could employ a method that would establish whether or not it is at the outset is fundamentally questionable. Hare seems to regard the typical 'German philosopher' as going about his business in the *wrong* way because he is prepared to use words whose meaning is (at best) not clear. And it is certainly true that Heidegger is willing to do just that. But for Heidegger, at the start of the inquiry, this 'being prepared to use words whose meaning is unclear' is a state of affairs that the inquirer experiences as strictly *undeniable* and not a reflection of an inquirer who is somehow *unconscientious* – and that shifts the weight of the observation. That is, it is no longer a criticism of a philosophical inquiry but an affirmation of its first condition. It is, Heidegger thinks, precisely because the meaning of Being is 'in some way' available to us and yet cannot be brought to concepts without more ado that he wants to undertake 'an investigation of the meaning of Being'. Whether the subsequent inquiry repays that opening wager requires an engagement with the text that Hare is unwilling to make.[36]

Of course, even this tiny detour into the opening of Heidegger's 'long and difficult book' goes beyond anything attempted by Hare in his essay. And so the real trouble with his charges against 'German philosophy' is not merely that we are not told who he is talking about (there are, as we know, various usual suspects in this game) but that not one example is actually presented as an illustration. Thus, like Ryle, the development or demonstration of the idea of philosophical division remains vague and free-floating. As I put it in the opening paragraph of the Introduction to the *Edinburgh Encyclopedia of Continental philosophy*, it would seem that it '*lives* on being free-floating'. It is, surely, highly revealing that Hare declares Oxford philosophers to 'find it hard to discuss philosophy with, *or to read the books of*, people who do not even seem worried about convincing the sceptic that their philosophical propositions mean something'.[37] It seems then that the very idea of a distinctive (but disastrous) 'German' (or, as we now more typically have it, 'Continental') way of pursuing philosophy, can survive only as long as the thinkers and themes which are placed under it are not only supposed not worth reading but, in fact, *are not seriously read*. What Hare calls 'the essential books'[38] (books that achieve a 'must read' status for Oxford philosophers) are, he states, likely to be those that are 'short, clear and to the point'.[39] Well, it is a fair cop. Kant, Hegel, Husserl, Heidegger, Sartre, Merleau-Ponty and many others on the list all wrote 'long and difficult books'. But if one is particularly pushed for time one could at least try to read the beginning, no? In any case, as I argued in Chapter 2, it is deeply unsatisfactory, *philosophically* unsatisfactory, to give the elbow to work in philosophy only on the basis of the fact that you find it hard to read. When Hare notes that he does not regard it as a duty 'to read more than a few books which others write' and that the content of most of 'the essential books' is 'quite familiar from verbal discussion' one cannot help but wonder who is most keen 'to collect a private coterie'.[40] As we saw in the last chapter, Jacques Derrida defines the 'bad' reader in philosophy precisely as the one who is 'in a hurry to be determined, decided upon deciding (in order to annul, in other words to bring back to oneself, one has to wish to know in advance what to expect, one wishes to expect what has happened, one wishes to expect (oneself))'.[41] It comes down to this: Hare is really only happy reading work by an other who is, fundamentally, one of his own colleagues (himself).

Hare's unambiguously stated thesis cannot still be thought to be in good shape. Because 'German philosophy' is presented, somewhat like Ryle's Husserl, in such a crude fashion, and thus only by slipping from the 'standards' of 'rigour and honesty and clarity' which Hare officially (and surely rightly) upholds for philosophy,[42] he cannot be said to have demonstrated it. But, perhaps he has succeeded in showing something else: namely, that British philosophical gulf-seeking seems to interfere with (or allow philosophers to forget) philosophy's own virtues. I will return to this in the next section where I explore a more historically focused illustration of analytic gulf-seeking.

Warnock on Expelling the Alien

In his book on the idea of analytic philosophy L. J. Cohen notes that what he is after is not an explanation of analytic philosophy in developmental or historical terms but in exclusively philosophical and conceptual terms. There is, he states,

> a characteristically philosophical question to be asked about the analytic movement, in abstraction from any consideration of its personal composition, of its temporal ordering, or of external influences that have affected it. What counts here is the content of what has been said, not the date or author of its utterance.[43]

I am very sympathetic to the idea that it is thoughts and not thinkers that should concern us above all in philosophy. However, while any work of words must, if it is to function at all, be able to function beyond the context of its production, I am extremely sceptical whether one can really give an account of 'what has been said' which conceives such works in terms of an abstract content that is radically free of all contextual determination. For example, can we really achieve an adequate grasp of Ryle's discussion of Husserl's philosophy if we do not coordinate his utterances with, say, British cultural responses to the war against Germany? How else are we to read remarks about 'claims to Führership' with any rigour?[44]

Having said this, however, I do not want to imply that the modern category of Continental philosophy should be understood in wholly non-philosophical – say, merely historical or sociological – terms either. As I have mentioned before, I want to hazard the tricky gesture of calling my account of the emergence of the idea of Continental philosophy a philosophical one. I want now to lay out why I want to see things that way. The basic reason is that I think understanding the articulation and construction of 'the Continental philosopher' after the Second World War requires appreciating it as a recent incarnation of a fundamentally and classically philosophical figuration, a figure which has, since ancient Greek times, permeated and haunted the philosophical imagination: namely, that of the *Sophist*. In what follows I will offer a sketch of this philosophically configured history as it emerged in Britain.[45]

After the Second World War, the development and professionalisation of philosophy departments at British universities (including especially those at the older universities) had become so pronounced, the distance from the philosophical formations of the first quarter of the century so alive to those engaged in the subject, that the (now almost exclusively young) personnel began to talk of 'the revolution in philosophy'.[46] A history of this revolution was also emerging, and it told of the emphatic rejection of distinctively *foreign* ideas. Why this was so finds its classic articulation in Geoffrey Warnock's assessment of the development of English philosophy since 1900.[47] Published in 1958, Warnock's book appeared at a time when, as we are beginning to see, those who adhered to the name of analytic philosophy were passionately affected by the idea of its difference to other work going on in the subject in Europe. Adherents to the movement of philosophical analysis were also well on the way to becoming *the* dominant voices in academic philosophy in English universities. Warnock's argument gives a lively and vigorous historical expression to and justification for that hegemony. At the core of his account is an image of English philoso-phy which would not have been recognised only a quarter of a century earlier, but which is, to this day, a central part of analytic philosophy's self-conception. According to Warnock, 'most philosophy written in English [in the twentieth century] has been, for better or worse, and I shall not here say which, something vastly unlike most philosophy in other languages'.[48] This vast difference is, of course, the philosophical gulf with which we are now familiar. That Warnock's apparent judi-ciousness ('I shall not here say which') is *fundamentally* disingenuous is evident from the terms and tone of his brief discussion of the sup-posed exception to this gulf-riven state of affairs: namely, the pre-revolutionary, *fin-de-siècle* movement of British Idealism, the British movement which, alone, was *not* 'vastly unlike most philosophy in other languages', the British movement with which the new history begins and *against* which 'the revolution' is launched.[49]

In marked contrast to his treatment of the British philosophers who he considers 'most important', Warnock does not regard it necessary actually to present or discuss *any* of the Idealists' writings, not even in the massively abbreviated form I have given to the usual suspects. Instead, he considers it 'enough' to characterise them simply as advanc-ing 'highly and ambitiously metaphysical' claims about 'Reality'.[50] For a reading of their thoughts Warnock substitutes an attack on what he calls their 'characteristic manner of writing', confidently castigating their 'highly coloured rhetorical dress'.[51] In what is, rhetorically speak-ing, a rather thin veneer of objectivity, we are informed that a reader 'attached to the presently prevailing mode, and with the courage of his convictions . . . might well find the style of the Idealists almost unbear-able'.[52] Bosanquet, for example, 'wrote sometimes with an air of vague high seriousness, in which the serious intent was almost completely muffled by the vagueness. And in the writings of the lesser men solem-nity and unclarity seem to rise not seldom to the pitch of actual fraud'.[53] Similarly, Bradley's 'opinions' depended for their 'persuasive force' not on 'the relatively unimportant trappings of argument' but the 'artifice of their presentation'.[54]

What is so striking about this kind of dubious and frankly indefen-sible form of unsupported 'air-castle' criticism is that it is precisely characteristic of the gulf-seeking attacks on non-British philosophy from the Continent examined earlier. And this, I want to suggest, is no accident at all. The fate of British Idealism is precisely what precipi-tates the emerging focus on 'Continental philosophy'. The coming into view of this new focus is nicely captured by a crucial aspect of Warnock's account, namely in his conviction that behind the 'ambitiously metaphysical' claims and 'vivid, violent, and lofty imprecision' of this species of 'British philosophy' lay 'German influences'. And these influences were, he states, 'very much an alien import'.[55]

The 'alien' status here is finely balanced between a national and a philosophical moment. And it will stay that way. In this irreducibly double voice Warnock declares that the philosophical movement of Idealism in Britain was never *really* British anyway. British philosophy was, he suggests, not long occupied with such 'strange things' before it freed itself from what the Idealists had called 'the main stream of European thought' and returned to what Warnock called 'the main stream of *British* thought'.[56]

At home, Warnock later revealingly reflected, the 'real campaign was already over' by 1948.[57] Henceforth, what British philosophy had for some time designated as 'Continental philosophy' begins to take on the role of that hated species of philosophy which is 'not deserving even of argued dissent'.[58] 'Continental philosophy' in its familiar evaluative sense is thus born, figured as 'exotic', 'alien', 'strange', 'vague', 'rhetorical' and 'literary'.[59] As British philosophy came to its philosophical senses, Continental influences were to be expelled and, where at all possible, to be avoided.

But were they? Or *could* they be? As we have already seen some of the most powerful and pervasive influences on English-language philosophy at this time were from, geographically speaking, Continental philosophers. So the picture of British philosophy coming home is never going to be factually convincing. Analytic philosophy has *numerous* Continental debts, and never even stopped engaging with writers that *it* calls Continental either.[60]

But there is another point to be made here which Warnock cannot really be blamed for missing, though it also dovetails nicely with the fact that the analytic movement never completely expelled the alien, and that is the movement within the analytic movement itself. Although it might not have been so clear in 1958, analytic philosophy itself underwent a profound shift in the postwar period, a shift from an empiricist phase to a post-Kantian phase. In a discussion of this shift, Richard Rorty lists Quine's assault on the dogmas of empiricism along with Wittgenstein's *Philosophical Investigations* and Wilfred Sellar's 'Empiricism and the Philosophy of Mind' as the major front runners here, and suggests that the post-Kantian phase 'began around

1950 and was complete by around 1970'.[61] I'm sure Rorty does not mean to suggest that there have been no further developments since 1970. Indeed, since the various kinds of philosophy that analytic philosophers have always called 'Continental' are all themselves, precisely, post-Kantian in their origins, the years after 1970 also mark the beginning of a period in which philosophy in the English-speaking world has been able to become (at least in its own post-Kantian parts[62]) somewhat less obsessed by the idea of a radical division in the philosophical culture. Gulf-seeking rhetoric has not disappeared, not at all, but it is far less powerful and less persuasive than it had been a generation earlier. Hence it is with some justice that Rorty concludes by imagining 'a future in which the tiresome "analytic-Continental split" is looked back upon as an unfortunate, temporary breakdown in communication'.[63] What I am trying to show in this book is that the very terms that philosophers have found to articulate that breakdown belong to it. I also regard the argument of this book as making a contribution to the further dismantling of the culture in which that breakdown flourished.

In fact, then, not only is it a mistake to think that 'alien influences' were ever fully expelled, the image of British philosophers coming to their empiricist senses after a brief dabble in Continental waters cannot now be sustained with any plausibility either. The historical 'blip' was not the flirtation with post-Kantianism, but the return to empiricism.[64]

Despite itself, I think that Warnock's history gives an eye-opening insight into why 'Continental philosophy' became the tag for the kind of 'self-indulgent blather' which seemed to threaten the very *raison d'être* of philosophy.[65] However, on its own it does not explain analytic philosophy's postwar *emphasis* on it, the apparent need or desire on the part of English-speaking philosophical analysts for a part which is their distinctive '*not-part*': something which, as it were, is retained firmly within it *as* something that must at all costs be *excluded*. I think this can be explained, and I think Derrida put his finger on it when he noted in the context of a series of not very happy exchanges with the American analytic philosopher John Searle that 'no one will be astonished when I observe that the Sophists haunt our present debate'.[66] No one would be astonished given the way Derrida is reviled by most analytic philosophers, but I want to see this figure haunting the analytic movement's understanding of the idea of Continental philosophy more generally. For the Sophists provide us with the very image of what psychoanalysis calls 'incorporation' that is philosophy's own.[67] It is the image of that which is *internally* or *philosophically foreign to philosophy*: that which threatens philosophy *from within*, and hence which *must* be kept outside. The Sophist is not just other than the Philosopher proper. The Sophist is the Philosopher's own Other. Now, in virtue of the particular circumstances of its emergence, English philosophy in the postwar period situated the philosophically 'foreign' thinking that must be banished as that mode of philosophy which had retreated back to its geographically 'foreign' soil on the Continent. It was there that philosophy was still practised in ways which constitute a threat to the (properly professional) philosopher. So 'Continental philosophy' became the insider's own outsider, and was represented in a convincing but free-floating conviction of a philosophical gulf in contemporary philosophy between what came to be called the analytic and Continental modes of doing philosophy.

But as should now be clear this is not a well grounded view. Indeed, it is a rotten view. This is not simply because there are works by some of the usual suspects which are not so very different to their analytic relations (although, as I have already indicated, this is the case), but because the very idea of pursuing work *in* Continental philosophy arises not though the (perhaps rather rough) identification from 'over here' of other philosophical traditions (that to some extent really were) going on 'over there', but through the projection as Other to analytic philosophy of a troubling possibility that *constantly threatens* what is going on 'over here'. That is, in my view, the idea of Continental philosophy as a bad philosophical road developed through a *false personification* of (every) philosophy's own *interminable possibility*: the possibility of failure and emptiness most famously figured as the Sophist. Paradoxically, and sadly, its effect occasioned just that possibility. As we have seen, at *defining* moments analytic philosophy has been able to fail as philosophy. This, I believe, is what happens when analytic philosophers condemn thinkers as irrational and obscurantist without taking the trouble properly to read or argue with them. The personification of an internal possibility as an external (and literally) foreign body gave analytic philosophy the false assurance that it was, in principle, 'healthy' philosophy. But what it was trying to expel could not possibly be expelled: *qua* possibility, it belongs to the very essence of philosophical investigations as such.

So taking our bearings from the discussion to this point, what then *is* Continental philosophy? Not, I would suggest, a style or method of philosophy, nor even a set of such styles or methods, but, first of all, the

Other of analytic philosophy: not a tradition of philosophy that one might profitably contrast with analytic philosophy, not a distinctive way of going on in philosophy, but a free-floating construction which gives analytic philosophy the illusory assurance that it has methodologically secured itself from 'sophistry and illusion'. Because of the reference to Hume here one might call this methodological assumption the fourth (and I would think finally final) dogma of empiricism: it is the dogma that one could possibly pursue philosophy in a manner that is free of that threat, the idea of a method which, in Wittgenstein's words, could once and for all 'bring philosophy peace'.[68] In any case, with this assumption in place Continental philosophy begins to emerge in the second half of the twentieth century as analytic philosophy's Other. And it is true: the primary texts of Continental philosophy are *not* works of analytic philosophy. They *are* something *other* than analytic philosophy. However, they are other to analytic philosophy without being reducible to *its* (own) Other.

The three examples of philosophical gulf-seeking just reviewed might be thought more frivolous than serious. But the impact of this kind of aggressive arrogance has been profound. The aim may have been below the belt, but they succeeded in their aim. Even if many, if not most, contemporary philosophers who think of themselves as part of the mainstream of the analytic movement would now accept that Ryle, Hare and Warnock, in these essays, approached their subject with cavalier indifference to the usual standards of exegetical accuracy and fairness, this may not be thought fundamentally to diminish the adequacy of their basic thesis: namely, that there is a rift, *a philosophical rift*, in contemporary philosophy. It is not only philosophers in the analytic movement who might accept this thesis. In the postwar era, anyone in the English-speaking world with a serious working interest in some one or other of the usual suspects will have been made aware very quickly that what they are reading is 'Continental' stuff that is regarded as 'out' as far as most analytic philosophers were concerned. So it is perhaps not entirely surprising that those who were taking seriously writings that the analytic mainstream were treating as beyond the pale began to take sides themselves. It is to the view from those working on the margins of philosophy in the English-speaking world, the view formed by those who developed a serious working interest in authors situated as 'out' by the analytic movement and who eventually came to appropriate the title of Continental philosophy for themselves, that I will now turn.

Notes

1. Gilbert Ryle, 'Phenomenology versus *The Concept of Mind*', in *Collected Papers*, London: Hutchinson, 1971, p. 182.
2. Jonathan Rée's 'English Philosophy in the Fifties', *Radical Philosophy*, 65 (1993) provides an excellent overview of the cultural environment in England at this time. A rather overambitious but often helpful discussion of the American scene at the same time, already drawn on in passing, is John McCumber's *Time in the Ditch: American Philosophy and the McCarthy Era*, Evanston, IL: Northwestern University Press (2001). I will discuss McCumber's account in detail in Chapter 5.
3. As I have mentioned already, there has been, as Donald Gillies noted, a 'definite shift' in the formation of the contemporary philosophical culture that means that this understanding is definitely *less* with us today than it used to be. I will return to this in Chapter 6 and in the Appendix.
4. Gilbert Ryle, 'Phenomenology versus *The Concept of Mind*', p. 181.
5. Maurice Merleau-Ponty, *Texts and Dialogues with Merleau-Ponty*, eds H. Silverman and J. Barry, New York: Humanities Press, 1992, p. 59.
6. Maurice Merleau-Ponty, *Texts and Dialogues with Merleau-Ponty*, p. 61.
7. Gilbert Ryle, 'Phenomenology versus *The Concept of Mind*', pp. 181–2.
8. 'I have grown up, as it were, studying philosophy at Oxford when Ryle was the king. He had a tremendous influence' (Michael Dummett interviewed by Fabrice Pataut, *Philosophical Investigations*, vol. 19, no. 1, 1996, p. 10).
9. Maurice Merleau-Ponty, *Texts and Dialogues with Merleau-Ponty*, p. 60. In fact, Ryle's claim that Husserl *assimilates* philosophy to science is *massively* wide of the mark, and he knows it. As Ryle himself notes elsewhere, that Husserl calls phenomenology a 'science' is not an assimilation at all but only (for English ears) 'an awkward terminological innovation' (Gilbert Ryle, 'Phenomenology', in *Collected Papers*, p. 168). Husserl wanted to regard his work in phenomenology as a 'rigorous science' as opposed to what he called 'picture book phenomenology' which describes the passing flow of experience in the natural attitude. But he completely agrees with Ryle that philosophy is not *in any part* a 'science' in the sense of the natural sciences.
10. Ray Monk 'Bertrand Russell's Brainchild', *Radical Philosophy*, 78, 1996, p. 3. For further information on some of the points raised in this quotation, see Van Breda's reply to Ryle in *Text and Dialogues with Merleau-Ponty*, pp. 59–60.
11. Bernard Williams delightfully complains that the analytic/Continental contrast is objectionable not only because the titles are 'obscure' and 'misleading' but because they involve a ridiculous cross-classification, 'rather as though one divided cars into front-wheel drive and Japanese' (Bernard Williams, 'Contemporary Philosophy: A Second Look', in *The Blackwell Companion to Philosophy*, eds N. Bunnin and E. P. Tsui-James, Oxford: Blackwell, 1996, p. 25). My view is that the situation is worse still. It is rather as though, with Jeremy Clarkson, one took cars to be normative for vehicles in general: one takes the terms used for describing the

construction and styling of cars to provide the standards appropriate for describing vehicles in general, so that whenever a (subsequently) 'non-standard' vehicle is found it shows itself as a *defective* car. *Even vehicles that are really quite like cars* – for example vans – will look like poor cars.

12. Maurice Merleau-Ponty, *Texts and Dialogues with Merleau-Ponty*, p. 65.
13. L. J. Cohen, *The Dialogue of Reason: An Analysis of Analytic Philosophy*, Oxford: Clarendon Press, 1986, p. 5.
14. Simon Critchley, *Very Short Introduction to Continental Philosophy*, Oxford: OUP, 2001, p. 35.
15. Maurice Merleau-Ponty, *Texts and Dialogues with Merleau-Ponty*, p. 69.
16. Gilbert Ryle, 'Phenomenology versus *The Concept of Mind*', p. 188.
17. A version of the lecture was published as an article under the title 'A School for Philosophers', in *Ratio*, vol. II, no. 2, 1960.
18. R. M. Hare, 'A School for Philosophers', p. 107.
19. R. M. Hare, 'A School for Philosophers', p. 108.
20. R. M. Hare, 'A School for Philosophers', p. 112.
21. R. M. Hare, 'A School for Philosophers', p. 112.
22. R. M. Hare, 'A School for Philosophers', p. 110.
23. R. M. Hare, 'A School for Philosophers', p. 113.
24. R. M. Hare, 'A School for Philosophers', p. 115.
25. R. M. Hare, 'A School for Philosophers', p. 111.
26. R. M. Hare, 'A School for Philosophers', p. 110.
27. R. M. Hare, 'A School for Philosophers', p. 115.
28. R. M. Hare, 'A School for Philosophers', pp. 112–13.
29. R. M. Hare, 'A School for Philosophers', p. 117. The basic challenge to the 'old ways' of philosophy posed by the Vienna Circle turns on the proposal that meaningful statements are exclusively of one of two kinds: they are either (directly or indirectly) verifiable statements about reality or they are statements which concern the role of linguistic signs. Nonsense is produced either (a) if one violates the rules of logical grammar or (b) if a logically well-formed statement is unverifiable.
30. Martin Heidegger, *Being and Time*, Oxford: Blackwell, 1962, p. 21.
31. Martin Heidegger, *Being and Time*, p. 21.
32. We really ought to be careful when throwing around labels like 'metaphysical'. Heidegger himself has a distinctive understanding of what philosophy as metaphysics is (namely, the investigation into the Being of entities). And (ironically, rather like Hare) it is something that he wishes to establish a distance from and, indeed, 'overcome'. I will come back to this briefly in a note in the next chapter.
33. With the citation from Plato that has lead some readers to attend to the fact that *Being and Time* begins 'in the middle of a Platonic dialogue' (John Sallis, *Delimitations*, Bloomington, IN: Indiana University Press, 1995, p. 99), Heidegger motivates a puzzle that, unlike 'the ancient philosophers' who found Being 'continually disturbing' and were 'perplexed' by what it means, we 'today' – we who have no answer to the question of what we really mean by the word 'being' – are not puzzled by it '*at all*'. It is for Heidegger a puzzle about the absence of a puzzle. A kind of 'riddle' (*Being and Time*, p. 23 [*Rätsel*, translated as 'enigma']): that (as

he wagers putting it) 'we already live in an *understanding* of Being' – yet we are untroubled by the fact that the *meaning* of Being 'is still veiled in darkness' (*Being and Time*, pp. 21–3, emphasis mine).

34. Martin Heidegger, *Being and Time*, p. 1.
35. Martin Heidegger, *Being and Time*, p. 1.
36. I develop this reading of the opening of *Being and Time* at greater length in *The Movement of Phenomenology* (forthcoming).
37. R. M. Hare, 'A School for Philosophers', p. 115, emphasis mine.
38. R. M. Hare, 'A School for Philosophers', p. 114.
39. R. M. Hare, 'A School for Philosophers', p. 114.
40. R. M. Hare, 'A School for Philosophers', p. 114.
41. Jacques Derrida, *The Post Card*, Chicago: University of Chicago Press, 1987, p. 4.
42. R. M. Hare, 'A School for Philosophers', p. 120.
43. L. J. Cohen, *The Dialogue of Reason*, pp. 6–7.
44. The relevant content may be, as here, cultural, or may just as well be a matter of recognising its textual debts and relations to other texts, possibly remote ones. The context I will introduce for understanding the idea of Continental philosophy requires just this kind of return to (the ghost today of) something remote.
45. I will address the distinctive American context in the final chapter. However, as the historian who has presented the most systematic (if, as we shall see, somewhat questionable) analysis of that context accepts, 'analytical philosophy first arose in England'. And my basic claim is that the '*philosophical* origins of analytic philosophy' are also the *philosophical* origins of the idea of Continental philosophy (McCumber, *Time in the Ditch*, Evanston, IL: Northwestern University Press, 2001, p. 11, emphasis in original).
46. In his William James Lectures delivered at Harvard University in 1955, J. L. Austin declared that certain contemporary (if, he interestingly notes, distinctively Kantian) 'views and suggestions' concerning the nature of 'many traditional philosophical perplexities' are 'producing a revolution in philosophy'. Austin also rather coolly says that we shouldn't find it 'a large claim' if someone were to call it 'the greatest and most salutary [revolution] in its history' (J. L. Austin, *How to Do Things With Words*, Oxford: OUP, 1976, p. 3). I will come back to that suggestion in Chapter 5; however, it is worth noting that Austin's remark about the revolution in philosophy may have given the impetus to the title of A. J. Ayer et al., *The Revolution in Philosophy* (London: Macmillan, 1957). That book has an introduction by Ryle and contains essays by A. J. Ayer, W. C. Kneale, G. A. Paul, D. F. Pears, P. F. Strawson, G. J. Warnock and R. A. Wollheim. Originally presented as BBC lectures, some of the essays look at the work of individual philosophers while others deal with schools of philosophy such as the Vienna Circle and postwar Oxford philosophy.
47. Geoffrey Warnock, *English Philosophy Since 1900*, Oxford: OUP, 1958.
48. Geoffrey Warnock, *English Philosophy Since 1900*, p. v.
49. The British Idealists comprise a group of authors who do not belong to the analytic movement but who do not, in virtue of their British provenance,

belong in the usual list of the usual suspects either. With due recognition to Warnock's description of them as getting involved with 'strange', 'alien' and 'foreign' things, they can, however, be added as 'honorary Continentals'. Again, my thumbnail sketches have been constructed by drawing on the entries in *The Edinburgh Encyclopedia of Continental Philosophy* (ed. S. Glendinning, Edinburgh: EUP, 1999).

Green, Thomas Hill (1836–82), British philosopher. Among other significant contributions, particularly in ethics, of great importance is his interpretation of the historical development of British thought. Warnock and others regard the turn to idealism as a kind of blip in the mainstream of British empiricist philosophy. Green insists that empiricists after Kant failed to observe the eclipse of their own thought. In particular, they failed to see that empiricism could not avoid making certain a priori presuppositions concerning the very ideas they were trying to explain empirically. His major work is *Prolegomena to Ethics* (1883).

Caird, Edward (1835–1908), British philosopher. Caird presented Hegel as a natural continuation of Kant's position. He also regarded dialectic, whereby opposites are synthesised in a higher unity, not just as a method of knowledge but an evolutionary pattern within reality itself. Caird attempted to elucidate the Hegelian notion of Absolute Spirit in terms which embraced religious conclusions. His major works are *The Critical Philosophy of Kant* (1877) and *Hegel* (1883).

Seth, Andrew (1856–1931), British philosopher. Seth was the first of the British idealists to raise serious worries concerning the seeming dissolution of individual personality into the Absolute. He insisted that selves be regarded as real and separate from each other. Seth also criticised the attempt to construct the world out of abstract thought, urging that this cannot account for contingency. His major work is *Hegelianism and Personality* (1887).

Bradley, Francis Herbert (1846–1924), British philosopher. Bradley argues that thought is not only the source of contradiction but the source of the explanation of it as well. The problem as he sees it lies in the fact that while reality is something concrete and unified, it belongs to the essence of thought to abstract and divide, and it is this that renders it contradictory and false. The ideal cure (which, as thought, can only ever actually be partial) is a holism without limits which would also overcome the distinction between thought and reality. His major work is *Appearance and Reality* (1897).

McTaggart, J. M. Ellis (1866–1925), British philosopher. His first works were largely devoted to the exposition of Hegel. His most famous work, however, is an attempt to prove the unreality of time. He begins with a basic observation: temporal language is divided into two kinds, the tensed (past, present and future) and the tenseless (before, after, simultaneous). McTaggart argues that the series of events ordered by tensed language is both fundamental and contradictory. It is, he argues, impossible and hence time itself must be pronounced unreal. His major work is *The Nature of Existence* (1921–7).

Other British philosophers closely connected to the major idealists include the political theorist and social reformer **Bernard Bosanquet** and the philosopher of history **R. G. Collingwood**. As I mentioned in the last chapter the later process philosophy of A. N. Whitehead, though not an idealist philosophy, has close affinities to the work of other 'Philosophers of Life' among the Continental philosophers, and also to Gilles Deleuze. So I will give him an honorary listing among the usual suspects too:

Whitehead, Alfred North (1861–1947), British philosopher. He is best known in the English-speaking world for his work in mathematical logic and the philosophy of science. In collaboration with Bertrand Russell he wrote the landmark 'logicist' text *Principia Mathmatica* (three volumes, 1910, 1912, 1913) which argued that mathematics is reducible to logic. However, Whitehead is among the usual suspects too because of his later work on process philosophy (and thus his relation to thinkers such as Bergson, Deleuze and Badiou). His most important book on this theme is *Process and Reality* (1929) in which Whitehead argues for the primacy of process over substance in nature: 'nature is a structure of evolving processes. The reality is the process'. Whitehead's stress on process is found in his major later writings including the following: *Adventures of Ideas* (1933), *Nature and Life* (1934) and *Essays in Science and Philosophy* (1947).

50. Geoffrey Warnock, *English Philosophy Since 1900*, p. 6.
51. Geoffrey Warnock, *English Philosophy Since 1900*, p. 6.
52. Geoffrey Warnock, *English Philosophy Since 1900*, p. 6.
53. Geoffrey Warnock, *English Philosophy Since 1900*, p. 6.
54. Geoffrey Warnock, *English Philosophy Since 1900*, p. 7.
55. Geoffrey Warnock, *English Philosophy Since 1900*, p. 9.
56. Geoffrey Warnock, *English Philosophy Since 1900*, p. 9.
57. Geoffrey Warnock, '*Mind* under Gilbert Ryle's Editorship', *Mind*, LXXXV, 1976, p. 51.
58. Geoffrey Warnock, '*Mind* under Gilbert Ryle's Editorship', p. 51.
59. One arrives in this way at the kind of table of differences between analytic and Continental philosophy that was sketched out in Chapter 2.

60. One might mention such things as the revival of Kant studies led by Peter Strawson and John McDowell's recent use of Hegel and Gadamer in *Mind and World*. Ironically, the very language of a national philosophical culture was an inheritance from Hegel.

61. Richard Rorty, 'Introduction' to *Empiricism and the Philosophy of Mind*, Cambridge, MA: Harvard University Press, 1997, p. 1.

62. There is, of course, a strong and growing naturalistic wing in analytic philosophy today (a further movement within the movement) that would want little or nothing to do with the post-Kantian developments in analytic philosophy that took off in the third quarter of the twentieth century. That movement in the movement is also producing shifts in the constellation of relations between differently formed analytic philosophers and those whose work lies outside the dominant analytic mainstream.

63. Richard Rorty, 'Introduction' to *Empiricism and the Philosophy of Mind*, p. 12.

64. Warnock's History: British Empiricism → Mill → German Idealism (blip) → Analytic philosophy. Rorty's Correction: British Empiricism → Kant → German Idealism → Early analytic philosophy (blip) → Later analytic philosophy.

65. John McCumber, *Time in the Ditch*, Evanston, IL: Northwestern University Press, 2001, p. 82.

66. Jacques Derrida, *Limited Inc*, Evanston, IL: Northwestern University Press, 1988, p. 42.

67. In psychoanalysis 'incorporation' occurs when something is retained 'within' *as* something excluded, *as* a foreign body which is impossible to assimilate and which must be rejected.

68. Ludwig Wittgenstein, *Philosophical Investigations*, Oxford: Blackwell, 1958, §133. Hume famously concludes his *Enquiries* with the following call to flames: 'When we run over libraries, persuaded of these principles, what havoc must we make? If we take in our hand any volume of divinity or school metaphysics, for instance, let us ask, *Does it contain any abstract reasoning concerning quantity or number?* No. *Does it contain any experimental reasoning concerning matter of fact and existence?* No. Commit it then to the flames, for it can contain nothing but sophistry and illusion' (David Hume, *Enquiries Concerning Human Understanding*, Oxford: OUP, 1975, p. 165). The first two dogmas of empiricism were identified by W. V. O. Quine as the analytic-synthetic distinction and the doctrine of reductionism (the idea that we can allot empirical content sentence by sentence) in 'Two Dogmas of Empiricism' (in *From a Logical Point of View*, New York: Harper, 1963). Donald Davidson identified scheme-content dualism as the third 'and perhaps the last, for if we give it up it is not clear that there is anything distinctive left to call empiricism' (Donald Davidson, 'On the Very Idea of a Conceptual Scheme', (in *Truth and Interpretation*, Oxford: OUP, 1984). As I say, the assumption that one can hope methodologically to exclude the threat of 'sophistry and illusion' could be called the fourth dogma of empiricism because of its nice expression in Hume. However, it seems unlikely that one can only criticise empiricists for holding to such an assumption.

5

The Continental Perspective on the Idea

Chickening Out

If what the postwar gulf-seekers in the analytic movement would have liked to have expelled from the midst of philosophy in the English-speaking world really had been fully expelled (*qua* actuality as it were) the story of Continental philosophy would perhaps already be a piece of analytical philosophy's mythological folklore ('There used to be some people who read that kind of stuff, but not any more, not round here anyway'). Of course, the fundamental argument of the last chapter is that what answers to the idea of Continental philosophy (the risk of 'sophistry and illusion') is not something that can be radically expelled from *any* philosophical tradition. *Qua* possibility it is a threat that philosophising must always risk. Nevertheless, the factual point, the fact that the effort to expel from 'over here' 'alien' ways of going on in philosophy coming from 'over there' was not completely successful, is *also* extremely important to keep in view. Analytic philosophy has become the dominant movement within professional philosophy in the English-speaking world. Yet during the rise of the movement not only did many analytic philosophers continue to flirt with various primary works of Continental philosophy, but a fair number of Anglophone philosophers and humanities academics have gone on to drink deeply at various non-analytic wells. And the story takes a new twist with the emergence of English-language writings that are principally (if not exclusively) focused on (one or more) primary works of Continental philosophy. With this twist we need to add to the contrast between 'works *of* X' and 'works *in* X' that I have been using up to now, the idea of work that is the *critical reception* of such works: we need to add the idea of 'works *on* works *of* (or *in*) X'. For, in recent years, many of the primary works of Continental philosophy have provided the impetus for secondary studies that aim to contribute to their wider dissemination and understanding. They can thus be fairly (if still perhaps misleadingly) identified as works *on* works *of* Continental philosophy.

As a matter of fact some of those critical contributions positively regard themselves as works *on* work *in* Continental philosophy too. As you can imagine I have serious misgivings about the wisdom of this understanding, but even so it is vitally important to understand why it came about. In this chapter I want to explore this appropriation of what I am representing as a thoroughly problematic title.

It makes little sense in this kind of context to try to identify 'the earliest case' of an Anglophone philosophical reader with a serious working interest in the texts of the usual suspects. However, we can say with some confidence that it is only since the 1970s that any such readers began themselves to make use – in both their teaching and their research – of the title 'Continental Philosophy' to identify their own area of interest and expertise. Why this happened at about that time is also reasonably well documented, although, as should by now be clear, given the history it was a rather odd choice. In order not to beg too many questions about that oddness, I want first to give the reason for the introduction of this title by English-speaking philosophers in a rather round about way. The reason, prosaically speaking, was this. In the English-speaking world there were (and still are) a number of professional philosophers with a serious working interest in texts by authors whose work was (and largely remains) not at all well regarded by most mainstream analytic philosophers. The course titles which were typically being used to teach the work of such authors included, among others, 'Phenomenology', 'Existentialism', 'Hegel and Marx', 'Hermeneutics' and 'Critical Theory'. These were all quite different (if typically overlapping) courses, but they were all beginning to look like explorations of authors and themes with increasingly more historical interest than contemporary relevance. By this I mean that the ideas explored in such courses were being challenged by many of those who they most deeply influenced. New trends and new thinkers were emerging that could not happily be included in courses going under those old titles. We can be even more precise here, for there is near universal agreement that the changeover to the new title occurred in order to enable teachers in the English-speaking world to include in the syllabuses of their various courses authors whose work was coming to be known, as Simon Critchley puts it, by 'the rather unhelpful and approximative labels' of 'poststructuralism', 'postmodernism' and 'French feminism'.[1] 'Continental philosophy', analytic philosophy's already-to-hand catch-all category, provided a convenient title for courses and writings covering both the old and the new.

I say that this convenient choice was, nevertheless, in some ways odd. Obviously, in part, this is because the new title – along with the rather unhelpful approximative labels that I have just mentioned – did not emerge from within the movements in philosophy that the new courses were aiming to cover. As we have seen, the reason why this title was to hand in the first place is that it had for some time served philosophers from the analytic movement as the name for a supposedly highly distinctive and seriously defective non-analytic tradition in contemporary Western philosophy. But, surely, one can appropriate titles and shake off trailing clouds of philosophical baggage and prejudice? That's not obviously so obvious. What is much clearer to me is that, in this case, the choice has served *also* to promote a seriously misleading impression, an impression which up until then only analytic philosophers had been seriously impressed by: namely, the idea that there really is a more or less coherent philosophical lineage or philosophical tradition that might fairly be called the Continental tradition in philosophy.[2] Well, I do not think we should be so impressed. Like John McCumber, whose own account of the division will be explored later in this chapter, I think the best one can say is that the primary works of Continental philosophy comprise 'a charming, motley collection of everything analytical philosophers dislike'.[3] In what follows I will show why attempts from those who appropriated the title for themselves to defend the idea that there really is a distinctive philosophical tradition in view here do not stand up to critical scrutiny.

Let me say straight away that even if I am right that the title 'Continental philosophy' gives rise to a seriously misleading impression of a more or less coherent philosophical tradition, that is not intended to suggest that teachers of courses going by that title cannot have a perfectly coherent idea of the thinkers and themes that they want to cover, and an equally clear idea of how those thinkers and themes relate to each other. The possibility of providing a respectable overview at this point is not, in my view, in the least problematic since the teachers of such courses will always be selective, and, as I have already indicated, the basic *raison d'être* for the new title was to enable these teachers to take on board recent developments and challenges to the ideas and approaches which they had been exploring under the old titles.

Nevertheless, I am saying that it is not seriously credible to suppose that one can give a coherent overview to the approach that belongs to works *in* Continental philosophy. In reality most people on the so-called 'Continental' side know one cannot provide such an overview.

Unfortunately, some think one can – or rather, despite more or less explicitly acknowledging that one can't, they nevertheless try to give one or go on using the title as if one could be given. Following Cora Diamond (on another topic) I will call this 'chickening out'.[4] And it is still rather common.

As the discussion of the various 'movements in the stream' in Chapter 3 should have made clear, anyone trying to put together a book on the idea of Continental philosophy which is more ambitiously positive than the one I am presenting here is bound to face a peculiar challenge of competence, and the risk of oversimplification and distortion is massive. By my lights, he or she must also face a more peculiar problem of principle, a problem that I want now to confront directly. David West puts it starkly right at the very outset of his opening chapter to his *Introduction to Continental Philosophy*. There is, he warns, 'a possible objection to our whole enterprise', namely 'that the isolation of a separate tradition of Continental philosophy is contentious or even perverse'.[5]

As should be clear, I am convinced that this quietly admitted objection is fundamentally sound. In my view, the real perversity is to suppose that there is a way (or that there are ways) of going on in philosophy which would seriously merit the title 'Continental philosophy'. However, if it is not to fly in the face of the entrenched, familiar and stubbornly undeniable reality of what Simon Critchley calls the '*de facto* distinction between analytic and Continental philosophy'[6] this point requires careful development and presentation. I will try to do so in what follows, but despite some complexities, the basic truth can be simply stated, even if it is extremely difficult to keep one's head above the water trying to adhere to it. In one way or another everyone can see it. Here is Critchley:

> It would not take a genius to realize that there are grave problems with the *de facto* distinction between analytic and Continental philosophy . . . Continental philosophy is a highly eclectic and disparate series of intellectual currents that could hardly be said to amount to a unified tradition. As such, Continental philosophy is an invention, or more accurately, a projection of the Anglo-American academy onto a Continental Europe that would not recognise the legitimacy of such an appellation – a little like asking for a Continental breakfast in Paris.[7]

And here is West:

> There is no single, homogeneous Continental tradition. Rather, there is a variety of more or less closely related currents of thought . . . In fact,

> Continental philosophy began life as a category of exclusion. Until recently the analytical philosophy prevailing within the English-speaking countries of the West . . . has almost completely ignored work produced on the continent of Europe since Kant – or, in other words, Continental philosophy.[8]

The difficulty of keeping the basic truth in view is very clear in West's comments here. He knows that there is nothing that answers to the idea of a distinctive Continental tradition, and he wants to acknowledge that the category originates within analytic philosophy as a term of exclusion. But to exclude something is not at all the same gesture as merely to ignore it, and as we saw in the last chapter it is utterly distorting to suppose that analytic philosophy can be even remotely accurately described as ignoring work produced on the Continent of Europe since Kant. Ryle might have liked to concur with West, but the fact is that the philosophical origins of analytic philosophy are *at least* as Germanophone as they are Anglophone.

So let's get things straight first with regard to the point about exclusion. As I tried to show in the last chapter, during the rise of the analytic movement the existing broadly geographical category of Continental philosophy came to function for analytic philosophers as the title of its own '*not-part*' part: the repository for the kind of 'sophistry and illusion' that is philosophically 'alien' to properly philosophical inquiry as such. Henceforth, the analytic movement appeared to be an essentially healthy philosophical home: the home of intellectual clarity, rigour and honesty. Continental philosophy, on the other hand and by essential contrast, came to be regarded as the home of obscurity, rhetorical excess and bonnet polishing, of 'wool-gathering and bathos' as Stanley Rosen has put it.[9]

I find it quite extraordinary that, having just acknowledged the crucial point about exclusion and accepted the basic truth that there is no isolable or 'homogeneous Continental tradition', West immediately goes on to say that his book will be about 'thinkers who, in one way or another, work in an identifiably Continental mode'.[10] As I say, I call this chickening out. Perhaps surprisingly, given the forceful way in which he states the basic truth, Critchley chickens out too. That is, even while noting as clearly and as starkly as possible that 'there is simply no category that would begin to cover the diversity of work produced by thinkers as methodologically and thematically opposed as Hegel and Kierkegaard, Freud and Buber, Heidegger and Adorno, or Lacan and Deleuze',[11] Critchley too will nevertheless go on to insist that there is a way of 'dislodging the stereotypes' that can show 'how, after all, the analytic/Continental distinction [can] be drawn',[12] a possibility he affirms even more confidently with the claim that 'the notion of Continental philosophy can, indeed, be well defined and constitutes a distinct set of philosophical traditions and practices with a compelling range of problems'.[13]

It would, indeed, make things easier if it were so. And, of course, the mere fact that the category of Continental philosophy was not, in its origins, named from the inside does not by itself mean that it is not so. It could have been the case that there was a tradition or a distinctive and internally related set of traditions to be identified, and analytic philosophers identified it. Analytic philosophers may typically loathe it, 'ignore' and 'dismiss' it; others, on the other hand, may come to find it 'compelling', comprising a well defined set of philosophical traditions and practices that contains 'some of the best of what has been thought on the philosophically most fertile territory on the globe for the past two hundred years'.[14] On this hypothesis the attitude is irrelevant, what matters is that there is, as West puts it, 'an identifiably Continental mode' of doing philosophy. And . . . isn't there? But *is* there?. . . But *isn't* there?

One wants to say that there is, after all, a distinctive Continental tradition, distinctive because certain things are true of it (or most of it) that are not true of the analytic tradition (or most of it). For example, Critchley suggests that one crucial mark of 'the Continental tradition' is that it 'would refuse the validity of the distinction between philosophy and the history of philosophy operative in much of the analytic tradition'.[15] But this way of identifying work in Continental philosophy is clearly unsatisfactory. First, if this is the crucial mark of the Continental tradition then there should not be primary texts of Continental philosophy (or at least not many) that *do* accept the validity of this distinction. But, without a doubt, *many* of the works that are counted among the primary texts of Continental philosophy (perhaps *nearly all* of them) would want to affirm the validity of *some* distinction between philosophy and the history of philosophy.[16] And so even if we read Critchley's criterion generously one would have to say that his crucial mark massively *underpredicts*.[17] That is, the problem is that his specification captures too little, so that many writings unproblematically counting as works *of* Continental philosophy turn out not to be picked out by the criterion that supposedly specifies work *in* it. However, if we take Critchley's criterion rather more strictly, and take it to require adherence to this distinction *as it is operative in much of the analytic tradition*, then it is clear that the supposedly crucial mark becomes totally empty because entirely negative. What we want is something like an idea or approach or distinction (or whatever) that is operative in much of the Continental tradition, but all we are being told is that the crucial mark of Continental philosophy is that it is not like (much) work in analytic philosophy. Not only is that not news to anyone, but there are an indefinite number of ways in which one may be *not* like something, and so the criterion says nothing positive about the supposed Continental rival. Of course, on my view (a perfect predictor by the way), a negative specification is actually the best one can do since it simply reflects the fact that the unity of the works of Continental philosophy is precisely a unity of exclusion. Critchley's criterion, however, gets us no further in specifying a positive feature of a distinctively or identifiably Continental mode. West (who we saw chicken out earlier) is, in fact, silent on the matter. Can anyone else do better? I know of only two that look like they might stand a real chance, and they do so in view of their clear appreciation of the fact that the Continental collection is, precisely, a 'motley'. The first I will look at is by John McCumber, the second by Robert Pippin. Both accounts are significant contributions to our understanding of the history of recent philosophy and the fact that I think they are both ultimately unsatisfactory with regard to the present issue does not mean that I do not think they have much more to offer than I deal with here. As I say, both happily accept that there is no methodological or thematic unity to the primary works of Continental philosophy. However, McCumber may be thought to undermine my claims about why it stands apart from the analytic movement, and Pippin may be thought to undermine my claims about why nothing holds it together from within. Either way, they pose a serious challenge to the views I am defending.

An All-American Story

As my scattered references to McCumber's book, *Time in the Ditch*, should indicate I find his rejection of the idea of Continental philosophy as an internally connected tradition or set of traditions fundamentally congenial. Like me, McCumber presents Continental philosophy as the 'philosophical Other' of the analytic movement, something which has no more to hold it together than the fact that it comprises a 'motley collection of everything analytical philosophers dislike'.[18] He offers a nicely Hegelian way of construing 'Continental philosophy' as the distinctive '*not-part*' part of analytic philosophy:

> The analytical-Continental split . . . is not really a split but a distribution, an assignment of complementary values. The two sides of a split are, after all, more or less equal. But that is not the case with analytical and Continental philosophy, which seem to have been assigned the status of 'essence' and 'accident', respectively. Hegel argued in his *Logic* that when one thing establishes itself as the essence of something else, as the fixed and definitive formula for what that something else is, there is always in that latter something of a residuum that, since it is excluded from the essence, can only show up (*scheinen*) as a passing play of accidents.[19]

I like this idea and, in general, there is much I agree with in his account. However, there is a dimension of his approach to the dominance of analytic philosophy in America – a dominance which made it possible for *analytic philosophy* to try to establish itself as the 'essence' of *philosophy* as such – which is no part of the story I have been telling so far. McCumber's central thesis is that the dominance of analytic philosophy in America is explained, at least in part, by the fact that it offered a way philosophy could be pursued which would conform to how 'Joe McCarthy's academic henchmen would have wanted it to be'.[20] The principal henchman here is one Raymond B. Allan, President of the University of Washington during the early 1950s, a man who became the 'foremost articulator of academic McCarthyism'.[21] Allan made it clear that he wanted professional philosophy to purge itself of any 'un-American' elements, he wanted it to adhere to strict norms of 'impartiality, objectivity and determination to seek truth',[22] norms which American universities have at their heart and which clandestine activity by communists and other radicals supposedly threatened. McCumber's claim is that this external pressure on academic philosophy paved the way for the success of analytic philosophy's efforts to focus on 'problems' and severely to *limit* philosophy's traditional and more ambitious emphasis on achieving a 'critical, reflective self-understanding'.[23] A dark secret of American philosophy then comes into view: the rise to dominance of analytic philosophy in the 1950s was not only simultaneous with the McCarthy era but profoundly 'fostered' by it,[24] 'decisively shaped' by it.[25] This massively 'skewed the development'[26] of philosophy, giving an 'undeserved dominance'[27] to a distinctively *un*reflective way of doing philosophy, a dominance that allowed it to define philosophy in terms of itself and thus to give rise to Continental philosophy as its residual 'motley play of accidents'.[28]

Understood in the sense of finding intraphilosophical differences (differences of style, method or problematic field) to mark the split between analytic and Continental philosophy, I think McCumber is absolutely right to emphasise that it is 'one of the split's most embarrassing features' that there has been no success in construing it 'in philosophical terms'.[29] However, McCumber takes that failure to relieve him of the task of actually exploring 'the philosophical origins of analytic philosophy' and to follow instead the hypothesis of finding originating forces that 'may not be philosophical'.[30] Yet even if we accept that the origins of this kind of movement are *never* purely philosophical (in the sense that they depended *exclusively* on the force of identifiable breakthrough texts or arguments) I am not convinced by McCumber's suggestion that the 1950s was 'a sort of axial period' because a generation of philosophers capitulated to the henchmen of McCarthy and conformed to 'the spirit of Raymond B. Allen'.[31] It is far more plausible to suppose that the mainsprings of the movement of analytic philosophy in America lie with two factors *external* to it, with two European imports:[32] first, with the emigration from Nazi Germany of certain key logicians and scientific philosophers, and second, with what McCumber acknowledges as the powerful emergence of analytic philosophy in Britain where, he accepts, the movement 'first arose'.[33] It is the influence of academic philosophers of the highest calibre, thinkers of the stature of Carnap and Reichenbach, Ryle and Austin, whose arrival provided the impetus to the growth of analytic philosophy in America.[34] And that is at least in part a philosophical origin in an uncontroversial sense. As McCumber himself acknowledges, for example, 'Carnap's article ['Truth and Confirmation'] played a key role in the defeat of pragmatism and the subsequent triumph of analytic philosophy'. And, in case it needs remarking, 'Carnap was no McCarthy'.[35]

McCumber is no doubt right to think that the analytic–Continental split really opens up in the 1950s but to claim it is 'a relict of the McCarthy era'[36] seems to me to pass over far too quickly philosophical forces internal to the movement of analytic philosophy. As I suggested in the last chapter, this is not a matter of feeling the pinch of contemporary external pressures but from what Arthur Murphy, President of the APA, in 1950 called 'the enemy within ourselves',[37] an enemy defined in terms of philosophy succumbing to ways of thinking undisciplined by habits of 'rationally self-controlled behaviour':[38] the threat, in short, of 'sophistry and illusion'. The philosophical vitality of early analytic philosophy lay in its ambition to 'overcome meta-physics', to overcome ways of going on in philosophy that, so the story goes, get on without argument and fail to acknowledge the logically prior question of whether their 'statements' on 'metaphysical' topics actually 'mean something'.[39] And of course something of this impulse is evident in McCumber's concern that analytic philosophy can *fail* to deal fairly with philosophers whose work lies outside the analytic mainstream, evident too in his insistence that his own investigations should be conducted 'in a reasonable and non-partisan way'.[40] The 'enemy within ourselves' is precisely a threat to philosophy from within philosophy, not a McCarthyite concern with un-American activities and leftist intellectuals.

However, instead of taking the perception of such a threat at face value, and recognising them as philosophy's acknowledgement of its internal condition, McCumber places them outside philosophy as indications of pressure coming to philosophy from 'the anti-intellectualism of the McCarthy era'.[41] Not only does this run against the grain of the texts he is reading but it leaves utterly unexplained why it was that 'Continental philosophy' became the tag for that threat, why it became the favoured name of the Other of analytic philosophy. I have suggested that to understand this we cannot avoid getting caught up with its British origins. McCumber, however, explicitly leaves attention to the rise of the analytic movement in Britain to 'others'.[42] In my view he thereby leaves out factors *fundamental* to his own story. Clearly one cannot understand analytic philosophy's emergence as a philosophy that contrasts with Continental philosophy in terms of McCarthyism. And what I have tried to show is that this contrast is inseparable from the perceived threat from what McCumber himself calls 'self-indulgent blather'.[43] *That* for philosophy *is* 'the enemy within', and for reasons that are fundamentally connected to the rise of the analytic movement in Britain at the turn of the nineteenth century it was philosophy from the Continent of Europe that came to be (mis)represented as that enemy.

In the end I think that the idea that American philosophers pursued the kind of philosophy 'that they were told . . . to do' is as 'wildly overblown' as Rorty's idea (if it is Rorty's idea) that philosophy can simply escape its cultural context and 'vocabulary'.[44] McCumber cites Harold Bloom suggesting that McCarthyism 'had no effect whatsoever on curriculum or appointments'.[45] That may be unlikely as well. However, the idea that philosophy has some 'dark'[46] and 'repressed family secret'[47] around which there is 'a general absence of discussion'[48] seems to me far more profoundly unlikely. McCumber's appeal to the proverbial unacknowledged 'elephant in the living room' is indeed a good comparison for his theory.[49] But one has to remember that if one is faced with a family who *never* mention elephants, that may well be, and is indeed, prima facie evidence for, an elephantless house. And so rather than wish that American philosophers would 'break their strange silence'[50] regarding their dark family secret one might be tempted to take them at their more than sufficiently vocal word: analytic philosophy in America, as in Britain, arose as 'a revolutionary movement', and for its followers its great success, its achievement of cultural dominance in the English-speaking world, makes the present 'one of the great eras in philosophy'.[51] There is in this, as I have suggested all along, some darkness – but there is no secret. The dominance of analytic philosophy for those who pursue it is simply its due, it is a function of its massive *superiority* over other kinds of philosophy.[52] I think one would be very hard pushed indeed to see a McCarthyite elephant lingering anywhere here. American philosophers in the twentieth century were not turning to analytic philosophy because they were doing what they were being told to do by outsiders but because they positively preferred this new philosophy over other kinds of philosophy from which it was distinguishing itself.[53] Nevertheless, and here is the dark side of this story, one of the fundamental facts about this movement of self-differentiation as it took place in America is, as Hilary Putnam notes, that, like their British counterparts and with the metaphilosophical import that has its British origins writ large, they became analytic philosophers by learning 'what *not* to like and what *not* to consider philosophy': the philosophical 'enemy within' was what American analytic philosophers too came to call 'the Continentals'.[54]

Ultimately, interesting though much of it is, I do not find McCumber's McCarthyite proposal convincing. As I say, it would be foolish to think that philosophy could pretend simply to escape its cultural context. However, for a chance to come to terms with that context in a way that might illuminate both McCarthyism *and* analytic philosophy *and* the motley that comprise the usual suspects of Continental philosophy I think we need significantly to widen our horizons. I would recommend that we attempt to take in what Robert Pippin has called the world of Western modernity as such. It is to Pippin's, in my view, astonishingly penetrating account of the modern legacy of the European Enlightenment that I will now turn.

A Classic Problem

As I mentioned earlier, Pippin's history of recent Western philosophy poses a significant challenge to my claim that nothing holds Continental philosophy together from the inside. For Pippin in his book *Modernism as a Philosophical Problem*[55] clearly identifies a genuinely internal trajectory of much post-Kantian philosophy from Continental Europe. It thus stands, in my view, as a particularly plausible candidate for giving a strictly philosophical specification of what might be distinctive about what we can identify as the primary works of Continental philosophy *from the inside*. I will argue, however, that it too fails to capture what it intends to capture, viz. a specifically Continental tradition in contrast to the analytic tradition. As we shall see, the problem with Pippin's view (unlike Critchley's on the generous reading) is not that it *underpredicts* but that it *overpredicts*. That is, the problem is not that his specification captures too little (so that too many writings unproblematically counting as works of Continental philosophy turn out *not* to be engaged with the issue that supposedly specifies work in Continental philosophy) but that it captures way too much – too many writings unproblematically counting as works in analytic philosophy turn out to be engaged with the issue that supposedly specifies work in Continental philosophy.[56] On the other hand, I take the error of Pippin's way to be profoundly instructive. In my view what Pippin ultimately reveals is not simply a feature of the movement of philosophy from Kant to the major texts of contemporary Continental philosophy, but the movement of philosophy from Kant to the major texts of contemporary philosophy at large. I want to begin, however, by highlighting a moment in an influential essay by Jacques Derrida that will help us focus on Pippin's basic proposal.

Towards the end of a long critical essay on the supposedly scientific status of the so-called 'human sciences', and at the point where he is concerned with Lévi-Strauss's assertion that a rigorously structuralist anthropological discourse on myths must itself be 'mythomorphic', Jacques Derrida insists on *not* ignoring the tremendous 'risks' involved with affirming such a view.[57] Specifically, he is concerned that the suggestion that the structuralist discourse on myth is itself mythomorphic is tantamount to asserting that 'all discourses on myths are equivalent'. Derrida continues: 'Shall we have to abandon any epistemological requirement which permits us to distinguish between several qualities of discourse on the myth? A classic but inevitable question'.[58] What is 'classic' about this question lies, I think, in its relation to the threat of scepticism. That is, the threat here is that any criterion presented to distinguish a genuinely 'scientific' study of myths from a merely 'mythological' discourse may itself be merely 'mythological', or part of some (possibly ruling) mythology. Maybe the whole of science or of philosophy or indeed of 'rational inquiry' in general is a kind of mythological projection, a narcissistic self-glorification on the part of 'Western man', without ground and without 'reassuring foundation'.[59]

Derrida's recognition of scepticism as a 'classic' challenge to philosophical reflection situates his work firmly within the orbit of the problematic that Robert Pippin identifies as distinctive to what he calls 'the modern age'. I want now to run through the central lines of Pippin's view in order to highlight its distinctive take on the idea of Continental philosophy. At the end I shall return very briefly to Derrida's own response to the 'classic' question.

For our purposes, it is of particular significance that Pippin develops his account of Western responses to Western modernity in terms of a division within the contemporary philosophical culture. Essentially, what Pippin suggests is that work that we now call 'Continental philosophy' comprises a wide and disparate range of diverse but characteristically *critical* responses to what he calls 'the claims of the official Enlightenment' or, to use the expression that gives his work its title, the emergence of a tradition for which 'modernism' itself becomes a philosophical problem.

It is, then, this modernity problem that would allow us to come reflectively to terms with our philosophical culture as characterised by a wide gulf in self-understanding. There is, *on the one hand*, a cultural self-understanding which is, as he puts it, 'founded on the scientific world-view and the political ideals of individual rights protection, a modern civil society, and democratic institutions'.[60] *On the other hand*, there are those for whom this self-understanding is 'a problem', representing 'a false promise, an ideological distortion, an expression of ontological forgetfulness, the will to power, or ethnocentrism, or a class or gender or race or culture bound strategy, all much more than the expression of a universally compelling, philosophically defensible, human aspiration'.[61]

One cannot fail to hear, in the variety of complaints made against those committed to the 'modern' self-image of humanity as liberated from ungrounded dogmatism, the voices from the movements in the stream which are usually – and rightly – located on the map of

Continental philosophy. And Pippin's account would thus allow us to see what holds these disparate groups together without trying to find a secret or underlying principle or family of principles. What is so distinctive and in my view so compelling is that in this account, uniquely in my view, we are presented with a *disjunctive* conception encompassing a 'diverse spectrum' and not a *conjunctive* unity of a shared outlook that identifies the distinctive Continental family.

Thus what is at issue, he is suggesting, is not a consensus over 'method' or 'project', but 'across a diverse spectrum'[62] a broad agreement concerning the *villain* of the piece: what one might hazard to call 'the spirit of our time', the spirit of the European Enlightenment which celebrates the idea that we have woken from our dogmatic slumbers and freed ourselves from traditional prejudices. In fact, for Pippin so widespread is this fiercely reactive and negative consensus that one could argue that the spirit of our time is itself very nearly one of 'self-hatred'.[63] That would be misleading, however, since that consensus is not sufficiently general: there is, Pippin asserts, a 'British and American tradition' for which 'modernity' is not experienced or encountered or understood as a 'philosophical' or really any other sort of 'problem' at all.[64] This, then, is the crucial issue that would allow us to identify a distinctive and yet distinctively heterogeneous Continental European tradition and a contrasting Anglo-American analytic tradition.

In Pippin's view, an explanation of why there is this division *within* the Western response to modernity will have to be historical in character. In his view the fact that the categories of Anglo-American analytic and Continental European philosophy are closely tied to cultural geography 'gives some sort of unwitting expression to the very different contexts and experiences out of which issues get to be or do not get to be "philosophical problems" '.[65] But whatever the causes, we are now in a situation where we are faced with a distinction between *philosophers who do* and *philosophers who do not* encounter the idea of modernity as a philosophical problem. Those who do can be identified with (potentially pernicious) Continental philosophers and those who do not can be identified with (potentially complacent) analytic philosophers.

At first sight, then, we have a nice (and nicely rough) distinction between those who do and those who do not experience modernity as a philosophical problem. However, as he refines his proposal, it becomes clear that Pippin does not quite hold this (as he insists too 'crude') view of things.[66] For, in Pippin's more refined view, it has to be acknowledged that *everyone* is in some way caught within the glare of the post-Kantian problematic he is concerned with, and that what he is identifying as the analytic/Continental distinction is really only a differential response within that common problematic:

> For many the philosophical issue . . . is simply whether there are or are not good arguments for the claims made . . . in behalf of the new way of ideas . . . For many others, however, such discussions often simply already reflect a number of modern presuppositions about what will count as a good argument.[67]

I want to look quite closely at Pippin's more fully developed formulation of his view in order to highlight what, to me, makes his identification of a distinctive Continental tradition look like a form of chickening out. For it seems to me undeniable that with the issue on which everything is supposed to turn (the issue with respect to which 'the general modern dilemma was fixed' for those who *do* encounter modernity as a problem) we do indeed find a problem deeply familiar to those analytic philosophers who, on the crude view, would not see a problem here at all. The issue here concerns the failure of Cartesian appeals to a benevolent God to remove 'the demon of modern philosophy, skepticism'.[68] So, if the idea of a distinctive Continental tradition is to be made out, the less crude picture of a still-roughly-two-way split in response-types to a generally recognised problem is being asked to carry a lot of weight.

For Pippin, then, it is the 'classic' problem of scepticism that poses the distinctive 'modernity problem' for contemporary philosophical self-consciousness in general. Pippin articulates the general form of this general modernity problem as follows: 'Given the self-understanding of an extreme break in the tradition, of a need for a new beginning not indebted to old assumptions, and so wholly self-grounding, the modern philosophical enterprise appears locked in a kind of self-created vacuum'.[69] On this view, wherever one sees an unqualified affirmation of the legitimacy of Western modernity 'the suspicion' that it is 'merely a self-defined assertion of will . . . will always be looming on the horizon'.[70] The ruling understanding threatens to have its grounds exposed in terms of its rule rather than its understanding. What is retained from the crude view is that our culture roughly divides between those who are inclined to side with modernity and those who do not.

Before we accept the picture of a rough two-way split here we first need to recall that, on the refined view, Anglo-American philosophers are in general just as much (or as little) fixated on 'the general modern dilemma' as any one else. The dilemma is this: confronted with the failure of Descartes' theological response to scepticism we *either* simply succumb to scepticism *or*, when we try to rescue ourselves, we make use of a method or theory which cannot be self-grounding, and so is itself vulnerable to the suggestion that it may just be spinning in the void. In short, the worry is that no demonstration of one's lack of dogmatism will ever be able to free itself from the threat of scepticism: any criterion one proposes will itself be vulnerable to the charge of dogmatism and hence itself vulnerable to that threat.

We find ourselves, then, with just the kind of 'classic' problem that Derrida identifies in his discussion of Lévi-Strauss. And for the moment all I want to insist on is that this classic problem is classic for everyone: the problem of trying to provide an account of the general legitimacy of our epistemological criteria, or, more ambitiously, for the idea that a scientific culture and open society marks a step forward for humanity is utterly familiar to philosophers in the analytic tradition. The slew of responses to it, responses that are more and less certain or confident of our contemporary condition, are the staple of every epistemology and philosophy of science course in the English-speaking world today: from naturalised epistemology to any number of foundationalist, anti-foundationalist, pragmatic, feminist, relativist and anti-relativist theories.[71] But now, and here I want to take issue with Pippin's representation of Anglo-American philosophy, to say this is just a matter of deciding whether there are good or bad arguments for or against a view fails fundamentally to acknowledge that the range of views noted above characterises a range of engagements with the issues that reflects what people genuinely *care* about.[72] I'll come back to this.

The initial ('crude') claim that the self-understanding of the West should be thought of as a philosophical problem *only* for the Continental tradition is clearly not satisfactory. However, what of Pippin's more refined idea that the real split concerns whether a satisfactory response to the 'modern dilemma' can *ever* be *supportive* of modernity?[73] Is the crucial point that, quite unlike the Anglo-American analytic tradition where we find (genuinely and with conviction) some people swinging one way some swinging the other, the basic characteristic of 'all significant [Continental] European philosophy after Kant' is 'some sort of *opposition* to the official Enlightenment understanding'?[74]

I think it is, without a doubt, true that *all* the texts that we can regard as 'the primary works of Continental philosophy after Kant' *are*

marked by 'some sort of opposition to the official Enlightenment understanding', opposition, that is, to the idea that a form of fully rational
and non-dogmatic self-grounding is possible. However, I do not think
this is a crucial point, but, rather, an essentially trivial one. In his effort
to avoid totally unjustifiably general statements, Pippin is careful to
specify his target very precisely here: the basic characteristic is 'opposition to the *official* Enlightenment' view. Pippin does this in order to
avoid the absurdity of excluding Hegel, and those influenced by Hegel,
from his set of 'significant European philosophers' after Kant. With
Hegel we do not have a philosophical demonstration of the failure of
Enlightenment modernity as such, but a particularly radical attempt to
reinterpret it in a way that allows us to accept the second horn of the
dilemma (the impossibility of self-grounding) without experiencing
that as an aporia that could be overcome only by appealing to trans-
historical principles of reason or logic which would certify our procedures and concepts as the right ones. And once Hegel is acknowledged
as writing in 'some sort *opposition*' to the '*official* Enlightenment', then
Pippin's attempt to use this as a criterion for distinguishing Continental
philosophy from Anglo-American analytic philosophy simply crum-
bles. Not only is it important to note that a great many authors – from
Marx to Critical Theory – situated on the Continental side are, like
Hegel, working 'within a still modern self-understanding',[75] but we can
come to see that the supposed mark of Continental philosophy (roughly
speaking its being 'officially post-Kantian') is more or less the mark of
'all significant philosophy' today full stop.

In short, as I suggested at the start, Pippin's thesis massively *overpredicts*. He may get the distinctive mark of Continental philosophy right –
but he does so only at the cost of not distinguishing it from analytic
philosophy at all. Not only am I comfortable with that idea in this case,
but given the disjunctive conception it is based on I positively welcome
it. However, Pippin's failure, in the face of the acknowledged 'diverse
spectrum' of positions, to show that there is, after all, a distinctive
Continental tradition makes his account of the split, refined as it is, just
another case of chickening out. Nevertheless, as I say, precisely because
it does so massively overpredict, because it tells us something about contemporary philosophy in general, Pippin's identification of the philosophical problem of modernity inadvertently offers us a crucial yet often
crucially obscured insight into the recent history of Western thought.

Let me conclude this discussion with some final remarks about
Derrida's response to the 'classic' question. While it may be thought

that Pippin's criterion (opposition to the official Enlightenment) is too weak, it might still be supposed that there is a more or less 'sceptical' dimension to the poststructuralist grouping that has dominated the 'new wave' of recent philosophy outside the analytic mainstream. Pippin certainly reads Derrida this way, representing him as someone who wants to *deny* that we can achieve a point of view on the discourse of modernity which escapes 'the modern dilemma', that is someone who appeals to the impossibility of self-grounding in order to *under-mine* all claims to be able to say how things are 'in fact or in truth'.[76] Derrida tries to do this, Pippin suggests, by insisting that all philoso-phy, and all epistemological requirements, are ultimately of a piece in that they are all 'essentially rhetoric'.[77] Not surprisingly, Pippin objects to such a proposal by pointing out that one cannot consistently defend this view without claiming to achieve the very point of view on how things are ('It *really is* all rhetoric') that it is denying we can achieve.

On this reading, one would suppose that Derrida would want to offer an (ultimately incoherent) affirmative response to the 'classic' question whether we should abandon all epistemological requirements that would permit us to distinguish between theorems and myths. That is, according to this Derrida, no claim about how things are has a more robust epistemic status than any other, and so ultimately *anything goes*. However, as Pippin acknowledges, reaching that conclusion depends on supposing that Derrida's affirmation of our general 'dependence on writing' (a dependence that Derrida identifies as unsettling official Enlightenment claims to autonomy and the idea of making a radical break from the past) can only be, by his own lights, just another rhetorical position (the rhetorical position to trump all rhetorical posi-tions). But there is *nothing* in Derrida's work to suggest that he takes that view of his own analysis of the conditions of possibility of writing.[78] Derrida does not think that engaging with questions on the relations between 'theorems' and 'myths' is a 'small problem',[79] some-thing to be resolved before lunch as it were, nor does he think one can investigate these concepts without their long-range history in view, as if they just 'fall from the sky'.[80] His theoretical work is, that is to say, deeply responsive to the (in his view, irreducibly) *aporetic* problem of self-grounding. However, his way of responding to this problem is not to turn away from philosophy but, rather, 'in continuing to read philosophers *in a certain way*'.[81] Derrida does not mean by this that he is no longer making a genuine effort to come reflectively to terms with our condition, or that he is reading philosophy in a way which slides towards mere literary or rhetorical play. Rather, he is on the hunt for those moments in supposedly modern philosophy where, for example, myths of illumination underpin claims to scientific or theoretical insight. More generally, as Christopher Norris has noted, Derrida's 'deconstructive' reading 'is strictly inconceivable outside the tradition of enlightened rational critique whose classic formulations are still found in Kant'.[82] Derrida too aims to help our modern culture free itself from certain myths of its freedom from myths, and he does not simply 'oppose' or 'reject' the values of the Enlightenment or *Lumières* in doing so, he does not wish 'to turn the page on philosophy':[83] 'That is not my "style", the "style" of my relationship to the tradition: I am not "rejecting" anything.'[84] Thus even the thinker typically presented as *most* sceptical about the Enlightenment, the Continental philosopher par excellence, is not the straightforward opponent of it that Pippin's reading would have us have it.

Of course, the initial 'crude' distinction was always too crude. But, and finally, isn't there nevertheless something to that idea? Isn't there something to the idea of an important division *within* Western culture between those who do and those who do not experience modernity as a problem? I believe there is. However, the distinction is not, I would suggest, one between analytic and so-called Continental philosophers. Rather, it is a distinction between those who attempt to come reflectively to terms with our supposedly modern condition and those who accept it without more ado. It is, I want to say, not a division within philosophy but a distinction between a philosophical and a non-philosophical relation to modernity.

Notes

1. Simon Critchley, 'Introduction', *A Companion to Continental Philosophy*, eds S. Critchley and W. Schroeder, Oxford: Blackwell, 1998, p. 2.
2. In an attempt to avoid the trailing clouds of disparaging analytic connotations, a growing number of philosophy courses in Britain today go by the title 'Modern European Philosophy'. However, if that title is intended to retain the idea that what is located within it is a distinctive tradition it only hides and does not resolve the problems.
3. John McCumber, *Time in the Ditch*, Evanston, IL: Northwestern University Press, 2001, p. 85.
4. See Cora Diamond, 'Throwing Away the Ladder', in *The Realistic Spirit*, Cambridge, MA: MIT Press, 1991. In that essay Diamond suggests that readers of Wittgenstein's early philosophy who attempt to hold on to the

idea that his self-declared 'nonsense' nevertheless gestures at genuine 'features of reality' are guilty of 'chickening out' (p. 181).

5. David West, *An Introduction to Continental Philosophy*, Oxford: Polity, 1996, p. 2.
6. Simon Critchley, 'Introduction', p. 3.
7. Simon Critchley, 'Introduction', p. 5.
8. David West, *An Introduction to Continental Philosophy*, pp. 1–3.
9. Cited in Simon Critchley, 'Introduction', p. 7.
10. David West, *An Introduction to Continental Philosophy*, p. 1.
11. Simon Critchley, 'Introduction', p. 6.
12. Simon Critchley, 'Introduction', p. 8.
13. Simon Critchley, *Continental Philosophy: A Very Short Introduction*, Oxford: OUP, 2001, p. ii.
14. Simon Critchley, 'Introduction', p. 14.
15. Simon Critchley, 'Introduction', p. 10.
16. As McCumber notes, it is a mark of what first came to be called 'Continental philosophy' in America that it was 'two decidedly *ahistorical* and *asocial* forms: as phenomenological introspection ['phenomenological investigation' would be a fairer way of putting this. SBG] into the structures of consciousness as such, and as a radically individualistic existentialism' (John McCumber, *Time in the Ditch*, p. xxii).
17. I am grateful to Max de Gaynesford for suggesting (from a very different context) the use of the concepts of underprediction and overprediction in this chapter.
18. Having said that, McCumber's book is peppered with references to thinkers who work in Continental philosophy and the book closes with a frustrating appeal to philosophers in general, 'analytic and Continental', to 'understand the strengths and weaknesses of their own traditions' (John McCumber, *Time in the Ditch*, p. 167). And after all that hard Hegelian work dismantling the idea too!
19. John McCumber, *Time in the Ditch*, p. 76.
20. John McCumber, *Time in the Ditch*, p. xvii.
21. John McCumber, *Time in the Ditch*, p. 39.
22. John McCumber, *Time in the Ditch*, p. 39.
23. John McCumber, *Time in the Ditch*, p. 10.
24. John McCumber, *Time in the Ditch*, p. 110.
25. John McCumber, *Time in the Ditch*, p. xiii.
26. John McCumber, *Time in the Ditch*, p. xviii.
27. John McCumber, *Time in the Ditch*, p. xxii.
28. John McCumber, *Time in the Ditch*, p. 86.
29. John McCumber, *Time in the Ditch*, p. xxi.
30. John McCumber, *Time in the Ditch*, p. 11.
31. John McCumber, *Time in the Ditch*, p. 99.
32. I am not suggesting that the springs are exclusively external. See note 53 below on Carnap's *pre*war experience in America.
33. John McCumber, *Time in the Ditch*, p. 11.
34. Ryle spoke on a panel with George Boas at the Eastern Division APA in Toronto in December 1950, under the general heading 'The Modern

Distemper of Philosophy'. Austin went to Harvard for a term in 1955 to deliver the William James Lectures – presenting the text now published as *How to Do things with Words*. He also took a graduate seminar on Excuses (using material later published in 'A Plea for Excuses'). Stanley Cavell recalls that Austin's 'material' and 'procedures' 'knocked me off my horse' (Stanley Cavell, *The Claim of Reason*, Oxford: OUP, 1979).

35. John McCumber, *Time in the Ditch*, p. 45. A philosophically nuanced presentation of Carnap and his relation to phenomenology and post-Kantian philosophy in Germany is given by Michael Friedman in his book *A Parting of the Ways* (Chicago: Open Court, 2000).
36. John McCumber, *Time in the Ditch*, p. 76.
37. John McCumber, *Time in the Ditch*, p. 4.
38. John McCumber, *Time in the Ditch*, p. 4.
39. I noted in the last chapter that Heidegger himself has a distinctive understanding of what philosophy as metaphysics is, and that this is also something he wants to 'overcome'. It seems inconceivable that Heidegger is not recalling the title of Carnap's 1932 essay 'Overcoming Metaphysics through Logical Analysis of Language' [*Überwindung der Metaphysik durch logische Analyse der Sprach*] for his own essay, written between 1936 and 1941, 'Overcoming Metaphysics' [*Überwindung der Metaphysik*]. For the subtleties of the Carnap–Heidegger relation on this issue see Michael Friedman, *A Parting of the Ways*, especially Chapter 1 where Friedman notes that *both* could be understood as appealing to a Nietzschean lineage here.
40. John McCumber, *Time in the Ditch*, p. 17.
41. John McCumber, *Time in the Ditch*, p. 14.
42. John McCumber, *Time in the Ditch*, p. 55.
43. John McCumber, *Time in the Ditch*, p. 82.
44. John McCumber, *Time in the Ditch*, p. 132.
45. John McCumber, *Time in the Ditch*, p. 108.
46. John McCumber, *Time in the Ditch*, p. 13.
47. John McCumber, *Time in the Ditch*, p. 18.
48. John McCumber, *Time in the Ditch*, p. 97.
49. John McCumber, *Time in the Ditch*, p. 8.
50. John McCumber, *Time in the Ditch*, p. 167.
51. John Searle, 'Contemporary Philosophy in the United States', in *The Blackwell Companion to Philosophy*, eds N. Bunnin and E. P. Tsui-James, (eds), *The Blackwell Companion to Philosophy*, Oxford: Blackwell, 1996, p. 23. Searle seems to me to want to be echoing the text of his former supervisor, J. L. Austin, who calmly noted that 'if anyone wishes to call [the present 'revolution in philosophy'] the greatest and most salutary in its history, this is not, if you come to think of it, a large claim' (J. L. Austin, *How to Do Things With Words*, Oxford: OUP, 1976, pp. 3–4). For a long time I found it completely baffling as to how this could be read as anything *but* a large claim. However, I now think that Austin is simply saying that this is just the sort of (as he says 'parti pris') thing that revolutionaries always say. So (and this is a wonderfully ironic twist) we should not regard Searle's semi-citation of Austin as making a speech act of the sort

111

that is 'a large claim' either, but rather as making a speech act of the sort that is an expression of his revolutionary zeal. Austin, always more consistent as a theorist of what people do with words than many of his more theoretical followers, is always one step ahead!

52. John Searle unequivocally asserts that, 'without exception, the best philosophy departments in the United States are dominated by analytic philosophy' ('Contemporary Philosophy in the United States', p. 1).

53. When Carnap arrived in America in 1935 he found that developments in philosophy in Europe had *already* arrived and that there was *already* 'considerable interest, especially among the younger philosophers, in the scientific method of philosophy, based on modern logic, and that this interest is growing from year to year' (Rudolph Carnap, 'Intellectual Autobiography', in P. A. Schlipp, *The Philosophy of Rudolph Carnap*, La Salle, IL: Open Court, 1963, p. 34, emphasis mine).

54. John McCumber, *Time in the Ditch*, p. 50.

55. All references are to Robert Pippin, *Modernism as a Philosophical Problem* 2nd edn, Oxford: Blackwell, 1999.

56. I think a similar problem undermines David Cooper's thesis that Continental philosophy is characterised by the distinctive ways in which it attacks 'scientism' (see David Cooper, 'Modern European Philosophy', in *The Blackwell Companion to Philosophy*, eds N. Bunnin and E. P. Tsui-James, Oxford: Blackwell, 1996). I have already noted a number of divergent 'movements in the stream' but I do think Cooper here identifies a very distinctive, deep and powerful undertow in the waters of the contemporary philosophical culture *in general*. My only problem is with his attempt to make it flow along the lines of an analytic/Continental division. The distinction between those who do and those who do not see philosophy as importantly continuous with or maintaining a special relation with science is, as I have wanted to acknowledge all along, a very important dimension of contemporary intraphilosophical differences, but I do not think it is contiguous with the analytic/Continental distinction. Heidegger's schema of the 'extreme counter-positions' of the ' "philosophy" of our day': '[Carnap → Heidegger]' may seem to speak for Cooper's view (Martin Heidegger, cited in Simon Critchley, *Very Short Introduction to Continental Philosophy*, Oxford: OUP, 2001, p. 104). However (and I think one can argue this point in both directions), one can only sustain the idea that the scientism/anti-scientism contrast maps onto the analytic/ Continental contrast if one reads analytic philosophy as far more steadily 'Carnapian' than it actually is. (Recall the variation on this point in Glock's table in Chapter 1.) My view is that the scientism/anti-scientism contrast does specify the most profound *philosophical* division in the sensibility of the contemporary philosophical culture in general, but I take it as deeply interesting that it cuts orthogonally across the standard analytic/Continental distinction. The reverence for the outlook, style and method of science is a regular *target* of some of the most influential work in analytic philosophy – and a desire to achieve the kind of status of a science is evident in a number of important texts in the Continental collection. For reasons already noted I do not mean to include Husserl in this

despite his effort to pursue phenomenology 'as a rigorous science'. I am thinking especially about classical Marxists and Freudians as well as certain Structuralists and Critical Theorists.

57. Jacques Derrida, 'Structure Sign and Play in the Human Sciences', in *Writing and Difference*, London: Routledge, 1978, p. 363.
58. Jacques Derrida, 'Structure Sign and Play in the Human Sciences', p. 363.
59. Jacques Derrida, 'Structure Sign and Play in the Human Sciences', p. 370.
60. Robert Pippin, *Modernism as a Philosophical Problem*, p. xiii.
61. Robert Pippin, *Modernism as a Philosophical Problem*, p. xiii.
62. Robert Pippin, *Modernism as a Philosophical Problem*, p. xiv.
63. Robert Pippin, *Modernism as a Philosophical Problem*, p. xix.
64. Robert Pippin, *Modernism as a Philosophical Problem*, p. xix.
65. Robert Pippin, *Modernism as a Philosophical Problem*, p. xix.
66. Robert Pippin, *Modernism as a Philosophical Problem*, p. xix.
67. Robert Pippin, *Modernism as a Philosophical Problem*, pp. 4–5.
68. Robert Pippin, *Modernism as a Philosophical Problem*, p. 24.
69. Robert Pippin, *Modernism as a Philosophical Problem*, p. 24.
70. Robert Pippin, *Modernism as a Philosophical Problem*, p. 25.
71. The uncanny proximity of analytic approaches to others here is perhaps most strikingly evident if we consider Quine's discussions of ontology, discussions which confront very directly Derrida's 'classic' question, suggesting as they do that the ontology of modern science is 'comparable, epistemologically, to the gods of Homer' and that the difference between concepts of 'physical objects' and 'mythological' concepts like 'Homeric gods' is one only 'of degree and not of kind'. According to Quine, 'both sorts of entities enter our conception only as cultural posits' (W. V. O. Quine, 'Two Dogmas of Empiricism', in *From a Logical Point of View*, New York: Harper, 1963, p. 44). Incidentally, if, with Simon Critchley, we try to frame the modernity question in *moral* rather than *epistemological* terms, and thus with reference to the problem of 'nihilism' (see Simon Critchley, 'Introduction', p. 11), the same familiarity with the moral sceptic clearly appears again. It should be noted, however, that (as before) whereas Pippin's view fundamentally *overpredicts*, Critchley's way of mapping things out (on the generous reading) *underpredicts*.
72. I develop this point at length in a discussion of the role of argument in philosophy in *The Movement of Phenomenology* (forthcoming).
73. Thus we should note that, whatever else he says, Quine is *unreservedly* on the side of science, and (on 'pragmatic' grounds) maintains that our modern world picture *is* superior by far.
74. Robert Pippin, *Modernism as a Philosophical Problem*, p. 44.
75. Robert Pippin, *Modernism as a Philosophical Problem*, p. 167.
76. Robert Pippin, *Modernism as a Philosophical Problem*, p. 173.
77. Robert Pippin, *Modernism as a Philosophical Problem*, p. 173.
78. I present the basic outlines of Derrida's analysis in an essay entitled 'Language', in *Understanding Derrida*, eds J. Reynolds and J. Roffe, London: Continuum, 2004.
79. Jacques Derrida, 'Structure Sign and Play in the Human Sciences', p. 363.

80. Jacques Derrida, in *Arguing with Derrida*, ed. S. Glendinning, Oxford: Blackwell, 2001, p. 104.
81. Jacques Derrida, 'Structure Sign and Play in the Human Sciences', p. 364.
82. Christopher Norris, *Derrida*, London: Fontana Press, 1987, p. 162.
83. Jacques Derrida, 'Structure Sign and Play in the Human Sciences', p. 364.
84. Jacques Derrida, *Arguing With Derrida*, p. 105.

6

The (B)end of the Idea

Reaching an End

John McCumber claims that there has been no success in construing the 'split' between analytic and Continental philosophy 'in philosophical terms'.[1] In this book I have attempted to succeed where others have failed. However, I have not tried to do so by showing 'how, after all, the analytic/Continental distinction [can] be drawn'[2] but, rather, by showing why, after all, it cannot. Yet so pervasive is the *de facto* distinction, so serious the breakdown in communication, that we find it hard to resist the idea that there must be *something* to the distinction. This is where it gets hard to keep one's head up, hard not to chicken out. Remember, all that one has to keep clearly in view, if one is not to chicken out, is that there is simply no category that would begin to cover the diversity of work produced by thinkers as methodologically and thematically opposed as those who are held within the Continental one. So why do we wind up wanting to say that nonetheless there is, for all that, a distinctive Continental tradition that we can contrast with the analytic one?

In my view, two reasons are powerfully operative here. First and foremost, anyone in the English-speaking world who has found their time *well spent* with thinkers regarded as 'out' by the analytic movement will quite rightly think of that experience as inseparable from their sense of what philosophy is and can be.[3] Second, there is no doubt that the various currents of thought that are brought together in the Continental collection are more or less closely related to each other. Now, I have all along been happy to affirm that a good deal of work in analytic philosophy is also more or less closely related to some of the texts that are typically deemed 'out' by analytic philosophers too. But that has *not* been the point I want to emphasise. I have wanted precisely to avoid erasing all differences within the stream of Western philosophy, and I have wanted all along to steer clear of the suggestion that what gets called Continental philosophy is really just analytic philosophy with a different dress sense. If we are not to mislead ourselves we have to acknowledge that there is something fundamentally questionable about the very idea of Continental philosophy as the name of a way of going on in philosophy.

And yet that does not prevent the title offering those who work at the margins of the analytic mainstream a collective home of sorts, an axis of solidarity for those vagabonds who do not confine their reading interests to writings from the analytic movement. In this chapter, I want to say something about being part of that axis today.

The basic argument of the last two chapters is that efforts to find an internal unity to the Continental collection will always either underpredict or overpredict because the only perfect predictor is one that acknowledges that the set comprises the distinctive '*not-part*' part of analytic philosophy: it is a unity of exclusion, not a unity of inclusion. Now, that is not nothing, not in today's world where if you are not part of analytic philosophy it can be hard to get a job, not nothing in a world in which your work is dismissed as rubbish without even deeming it necessary to provide argued dissent, not nothing when your work is systematically distorted and denounced in the same grotesque gesture.

But that is not all. In its rapid and impressive spread in the English-speaking world – and now beyond that – the rise of the analytic movement has been instrumental not only in defining its own history and character (problematically as we have seen) but at the same time (and in many respects far more problematically) the history and character of other kinds of philosophy too. So aggressive and distorting has this proved to be that out of a disparate series of movements in the waters of Western thought, it has managed to forge an axis of solidarity where there is, in fact, no unity of thought.

As we have seen, some have wanted to see in that axis a deeper unity of thought. Some have wanted the axis to turn a big philosophical wheel. Given the dominance of the idea of a division between the analytic and Continental traditions in the contemporary philosophical culture, the temptation to think this way may be totally understandable – and on occasion extremely hard to avoid – if, say, you only have a minute or two, or you are speaking to someone from the BBC or CNN – but that does not prevent it from being unjustifiable and misleading.

I think it is deeply significant that the idea of a tradition of Continental philosophy has its origins in and is part of the conceptuality of analytic philosophy. The peculiar difficulty this fact throws up for us today is consistently to acknowledge that what is non-arbitrary about the specific collection of thinkers gathered together under the Continental title is not something that can be unearthed through reading their work. In this chapter I will explore where this leads and leaves us today.

Enders and Benders

I have suggested that there are two basic reasons why people whose work engages seriously with one or other or some of the usual suspects of Continental philosophy today tend to think that there is or must be a distinctive tradition of Continental philosophy as distinguished from the analytic tradition. In conjunction with the fact that the collection of usual suspects is not a completely arbitrary grouping of utterly unrelated authors, the main reason here is, I think, this: that having found one's time well spent with a thinker or thinkers who are considered 'out' by the analytic movement, the experienced interest in that encounter strongly suggests the idea that there really is or must be, after all, this other 'Continental' way of doing things, this alternative way of going on in philosophy. What seems to me right about this is that, in the light of this experienced interest, one cannot (to partly borrow a partly borrowed expression from Stephen Mulhall) but find the 'picture of the essence of philosophical writing to which [most analytic philosophers] officially cleave as open to question'.[4] Once that picture has been challenged, the apparent modesty of the standard analytic evaluation of 'what it is for such writing to be well shaped and disciplined',[5] and so ultimately the apparently modest mode of its revolutionary inheritance of the subject called 'philosophy' can come to seem deeply immodest and distorting. As I say, that result can make it extremely tempting to suppose that there is an alternative non-immodest or non-distorting line of inheritance available for more open-minded or less desiccated readers. However, it seems to me important that one can fully affirm the result without needing to affirm the idea that there is such an alternative at all. I will explain this.

We need first to remember why it is that the origins of the distinction between analytic and Continental philosophy are not at all irrelevant to the status of the movements thereby supposedly distinguished. The idea here is that during the rise of the analytic movement the category of 'Continental philosophy' came to be represented as that which contains all that is *philosophically foreign* to philosophy, and so as what must be excluded by a healthy philosophical culture. I have called this the false personification of philosophy's own interminable possibility of failure, the attempt methodologically to evade the internal possibility that what one is doing might just be a kind of spinning in the wind or wool-gathering (the fourth dogma of empiricism). In recalling this argument Stella Sandford (an excellent reader of the usual suspects who is at times rather more confident about the idea of a distinctive Continental tradition than I am) interestingly adds '(analytic)' into the phrase where I simply talk about 'philosophy's interminable possibility of failure'.[6] That addition (perhaps unintentionally but still conveniently) holds on to the idea that one might inhabit a fold in philosophy that would have overcome that threat. And there, in my view, the danger lies. As I see things the problems really begin as soon as there is, as Geoffrey Bennington has put it, a 'fold of philosophers' who 'believe they really are philosophers and know what philosophy is and how to do it'.[7] Ultimately, then, in my view Sandford's affirmation of a 'self-determined' version of Continental philosophy, a version that would have freed itself from the 'disparaging' analytic idea of it,[8] represents a 'fold' only marginally less problematic than its self-authorised analytic opponent, and certainly has not escaped the threat of emptiness.

I will still say only marginally less problematic, however, since, as things stand, and for reasons I have tried to make clear, the outbursts of 'war-driven rhetoric', of 'denunications and even smears', which mark the 'discussion' between insiders and outsiders to such 'folds' today are, as Bennington notes, 'rather massively the case on the "analytic" side'.[9] I take it that this is particularly closely connected to the philosophically 'alien' status of the 'Continental philosopher' as constructed by the early movers and shakers of the analytic movement. As Bennington puts it, 'nothing is more like a holy war than the war of what perceives itself as reason against what it perceives as unreason'.[10] Nevertheless, it cannot be ignored that a war declared by the other can have the (perhaps desired) effect of uniting (or, as I put it earlier, *forging* a unity as) its opponent. One can anticipate that for the vast majority of those who spend time intensively reading work by (among others) the usual suspects there will be occasions when the felt need to countersign that declaration of war from and *as* the 'Continental' side is all but irresistible. As will become clear, I do not regard myself as somehow free of such gulf-effects. Moreover, it would be utterly naive to think one could totally control them. Much as it pains me to acknowledge it, it would not be altogether surprising if at least some of those countersignatories took wool-gathering to be an at least sometimes excusable way of going on in philosophy.[11]

In the end, this is why I think that (despite my qualifications) chick-ening out on the question of the very idea of Continental philosophy is not essentially more responsible than going in for the kind of 'air-castle' constructions of it that were once (and in some quarters remain) typical of the analytic movement. Again, the point is that as soon as someone attempts to identify something as a healthy or philosophically respon-sible philosophical home, for example as soon as someone appropriates the title 'Continental philosophy' to name what they regard as the site of the most fertile movements in contemporary philosophy, a distinc-tive tradition with its own distinctive principles, even 'first principles',[12] not only would that be no guarantee at all that one had freed oneself from the threat of having a good conscience, philosophically speaking, it would actually promote the reverse, for it assumes that this kind of health could become an instituted method, approach, style, idiom or some other mode of inheritance which could successfully expel the threat of emptiness. But that threat, I want to say, belongs (*qua* threat) to the condition of any philosophising worthy of the name whatsoever: it is not just something that we occasionally fall into (in falling away from philosophy proper) and from which a tradition or methodology or orientation might possibly secure us protection.[13]

I want to close my discussion with a few words connecting these points to the future inheritance of Continental philosophy as I see it. I have no doubt that there will be a continued and indeed one might hope growing line of readers and students of philosophy spending their time and finding their time well spent with (among others) one or other or some of the usual suspects. I expect to be very much among them.[14] However, for reasons that will become clearer shortly, it seems to me more or less inevitable that each of these readers will be riven by a conflict between two kinds of response to their experience, responses that could be figured as that of the 'ender' and that of the 'bender' respectively.

The ender is the one who knows (what is in any case obvious) that the very idea of a Continental tradition is 'contentious or even per-verse'[15] and so will be inclined to work with a certain lack of interest in securing or maintaining the idea of the analytic/Continental divi-sion. As should be evident, I am an enthusiastic ender. So is Simon Critchley. Along with his already witnessed tendency to chicken out, Critchley also presents Continental philosophy 'as a self-description' which may, as he puts it, prove only 'a necessary – but perhaps transi-tory – evil of the professionalisation of the discipline'.[16] Moreover, it is clear to Critchley that this transitional period may be coming to an end. There is, in his view, nothing special going on in 'Paris or Frankfurt' at the moment, and it would be a serious mistake to 'expect any new princes(sse)s from over the water'.[17] For Critchley then, and for myself too, one should not ignore the paths into the future which aim to cultivate ways of going on which will encourage our philosophical culture to overcome, as Critchley puts it in Rortyian vein, 'a distinction which has become tiresome'.[18]

This is not, however, the point of view that either Critchley or I will endorse at every turn. There is this other kind of response, the response of the bender, which always comes along too. The bender response demands that we acknowledge the *de facto*, real-world gulf or, at the very least, real-world gulf-effects, holding apart many whose work is marked by a serious interest in (among others) the usual suspects and many analytic philosophers. And the bender is (at least on occasion) willing to appropriate the title 'Continental philosophy' (perhaps with an additional and cautious 'so-called') in order to do so. When they are most confident (or most resigned) they know they are fated to remain 'perverted' in the eyes of most analytic philosophers, and they may well see attempts to find ways of working without the distinction as little more than an expression of 'a fawning need for Oxbridge acceptance', a need that they have 'long ago dispensed with'.[19]

I think these two responses, that of the ender and that of the bender, struggle within the breast of everyone who has become a serious reader of the usual suspects. For such readers cannot but find themselves embroiled in an inescapable, and rather singular, double demand or double bind.

On the one hand, the ender (in us) will insist that while one has to be careful not to fly in the face of the *de facto* distinction, it is equally important to acknowledge philosophical differences that do. In doing so I think one makes oneself responsive to a deeper, one might say 'constitutional difference' in philosophy: namely, between those who do and those who do not think they know what (inheriting) philosophy (philosophically) is. This difference is constitutional because we are all inheritors here, and as such we all inherit the endless task, the endless risk, of making what we do normative for philosophy. And we do so, everyone of us, as soon as we open our mouths to speak or put pen to paper. In the clear and decisive 'Oh, yes' and 'Oh, no' of a philosopher at home in his or her institutional fold, there may be few signs of anxiety. Nevertheless, while one can never simply do without philosophical institutions and their histories, the essential existential risk that is inherited with the (inherited) words 'I, *philosopher*, say . . .' will survive as such today only as long as it can survive *without* the assurances of an institutional guarantee – whether analytic, Continental or anything else.

On the other hand, however, one only needs to imagine talking about such 'existential risks' to a hard-nosed analytic philosopher to see one's utter inability to remain simply or purely philosophical through and through. And the bender (in us) will want to insist that even if one should never seek out or take refuge in an institutional guarantee, one is also never simply free of some institution or other either. Everyone who in their own way inherits philosophy is always also and willy-nilly situating themselves (deliberately or not, consciously or not) with respect to going institutions, valuations and folds. And whether one likes it or not, invites it or not, or resists it or not there are always police waiting in the wings, ready to intervene to place every(other)one.

What one might call 'lively benders' may thus tend to *de-emphasise* the sometimes deep methodological and thematic differences between philosophers outside the dominant analytic mainstream, and so are those most likely to chicken out. However, the contrasting case of the 'lively ender' is likely to be someone who is least affected by or who most wants (or needs) to forget the in-the-world conditions of philosophical identification. The point here is that the ender response no less than the bender response is always also engaged in a 'political' strategy, and is so even (perhaps especially) at the moment when it seems to transcend such vicissitudes and claims to speak 'purely philosophically'. An ender, even if not 'fawning for Oxbridge acceptance', certainly looks like someone who wants to get on better with the institutionally dominant analytic mainstream, and no doubt appearing in the world as an ender may make you more employable around here these days.

That being said, however, even if you are lucky enough to have a job, you are now less likely than ever to be working alongside many (if any) departmental colleagues with a serious working interest in your work,[20] and, moreover, you will in any case have a serious dearth of places to publish it and a critical shortage of institutional avenues of financial support for your 'conferences' and 'research'. At least the bender response is prepared for this kind of glass ceiling, more alive to the facts about institutional prejudices. No reader of the usual suspects can work in philosophy in the English-speaking world and be blind to the prejudices against them.

And so today, even in the absence of a Continental tradition to inherit or participate in, anyone who has found their time genuinely well spent with one or other or some of the usual suspects is a potential inheritor (whether they like it or not, invite it or not, resist it or not) of the going institutional risk that is inherited with the (inherited) (English) words 'This *Continental philosopher* says. . .', words which I know are there for any one to take (or, indeed, refuse[21]), in my own case as soon as I open my mouth to speak or put my pen to paper. No doubt whether or when or how one might want to take on the responsibility of using them for oneself will remain the singular existential-institutional question for every reader of the usual suspects for some time to come.

Continental Philosophy Today

In the introduction to a book which drew connections between two of the main (but largely independent) philosophical currents found among the primary works of Continental philosophy, a leading American proponent of their interest and importance suggested that what 'Continental philosophers' do in *America* today effectively defines what 'Continental philosophy' *is*: 'it has come to describe', he says, 'quite precisely what we do here in America'.[22] In all fairness, one really should open the stage a little to the British wing – as one would have said when the American text was written (1987), to Warwick and Essex as it were.[23] Nevertheless, it seems to me that this rather odd sounding claim is actually quite a good one, at least in part as we shall see. The idea is that the Anglophone 'Continental philosophers' are not marked (as some of them are tempted to think they are) by their involvement with the tradition constituted by 'the primary texts *in* Continental philosophy' but by the way they have managed to develop an alternative and distinctly positive *reception* of the varied succession of post-Kantian European writings that comprise the '*not-part*' of the analytic movement.

However, as we have noted even the most exemplary texts of this type are structurally secondary to the primary texts *of* Continental philosophy that they read. In a formulation I have found extremely helpful in trying to think well about the idea of Continental philosophy today, Peter Osborne, Professor of Modern European Philosophy at Middlesex University, sums up the strange but nevertheless distinctive situation we find ourselves in here, a situation in which, strictly speaking (and in marked contrast to what we find in analytic philosophy), *there is no such thing as a primary text* in *Continental philosophy*:

> I take 'primary texts "in" Continental philosophy' to be missing because, as a genre of more-or-less pure reception/interpretation, what we call 'texts in Continental philosophy' is work that mediates the relation of the 'primary texts "of" Continental philosophy' to another philosophical culture rather than philosophising with/out of/about them in a historically primary way. I take the 'primary texts "of" Continental philosophy' to be the primary of texts of post-Kantian philosophy in general in the non-analytical mode.[24]

While I see no value in supposing that there is a profound *philosophical* gulf between 'two traditions' within the contemporary philosophical culture, my attack on the very idea of Continental philosophy is not intended to 'sink the differences' between philosophers of various kinds, or (as Christopher Norris nicely puts it) to suggest 'in a vaguely ecumenical spirit' that they are all really 'saying much the same thing, give or take a few localised peculiarities of technical idiom'.[25] On the contrary, the central claim of this book has been that one cannot even say that about the primary texts *of* Continental philosophy. That collection does not constitute the primary texts *in* Continental philosophy but (with respect to the 'new wave' of Anglophone Continental philosophers) the primary texts *for* it.

So have we now finally found a good use for the idea of Continental philosophy? Should we in future confine it to the self-styled new wave of Anglophone 'Continental philosophers'? One could, and some do. However, in a paradoxical mirror of the analytic reception that sunk all the differences among the usual suspects, this other Anglophone invention also risks forging a unity of thought in a field that remains traversed by major methodological and thematic differences.

Thus, yet again, it is important to see that the construction of a division, here a division of the English-language reception context, tends to mask the profoundly varied forces of unity within the Anglophone field of reception, a field of variations which is easier to describe in terms of rough distributions of research interests related to 'proper names' than it is possible to divine in terms of rough methodological, thematic or stylistic commitments or characteristics. That is, while there is a spectrum of cases to be identified we still do not see here a spectrum of philosophical outlooks. What is at issue here is not a movement from the more to the less analytic but a movement from readers whose research interests are more or less exclusively concerned with work from the analytic mainstream to readers whose research interests are more or less exclusively with authors regarded as 'out' by that mainstream. This array can be represented by a graphic illustration of British academic philosophy in 2003/4 as shown in Figure 6.1.[26] (I'm sure something similar could be identified in America and Australia too.)

Note, first, that the position at the extreme right-hand side of this spectrum indicates only that analytic authors and resources are not the major focus of someone's research. It does not represent and is not intended to suggest that there is, at this point, a strikingly significant methodological or thematic or stylistic distance here from those typically found in the analytic movement.[27] Second, it should be remembered (how can it now not be) that there is a considerable variation of methodology and style within the group of seventy-six whose research is represented here that is not represented in this table. However, and all these variations apart, in the (b)end, something is shared by that group that is to my mind far more significant than what is not. And what is shared here gives us all a wonderfully perverse reason to be grateful for being set apart from the analytic mainstream. What we share is, in fact, precisely what has kept me in philosophy for the last twenty years or so: namely, that having struggled to come to terms with writings by (among others) one or other or some of the usual suspects, we have all found that, as Mary Warnock put it back in 1965 after reading Sartre's *Being and Nothingness*, 'it is impossible not to feel that

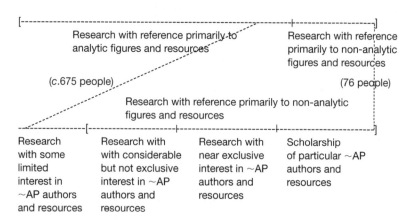

Figure 6.1 *Research concentration in philosophy in the UK 2003/4.*

the struggle was worth while'.²⁸ We, *we philosophers*, found it *over here* too, in (various different) texts that most analytic philosophers do not read and, as analytic philosophers, find it seriously difficult to read well. We (also) found the struggle worth while on (various) pages they can't turn. Both professionally and personally the struggle continues. I commend it to you.²⁹

Notes

1. John McCumber, *Time in the Ditch*, Evanston, IL: Northwestern University Press, 2001, p. xxi.
2. John McCumber, *Time in the Ditch*, p. 8.
3. They are 'ignored' in the sense that you ignore a turning on a walk when the guide book tells you 'You will see a path to the left. Ignore it'.
4. Stephen Mulhall, *Inheritance and Originality*, Oxford: OUP, 2001, p. 1.
5. Stephen Mulhall, *Inheritance and Originality*, p. 1.
6. Stella Sandford, 'Johnny Foreigner', *Radical Philosophy*, no. 102, 2000, p. 43.
7. Geoffrey Bennington, 'For the Sake of Argument', in *Arguing with Derrida*, ed. S. Glendinning, Oxford: Blackwell, 2001, p. 38.
8. Stella Sandford, 'Johnny Foreigner', p. 43.
9. Geoffrey Bennington, 'For the Sake of Argument', p. 41.
10. Geoffrey Bennington, 'For the Sake of Argument', p. 41.
11. Simon Critchley identifies the 'worst excesses' of what he finds in analytic philosophy and so-called Continental philosophy as 'scientism' and 'obscurantism' respectively (Simon Critchley, *Very Short Introduction to Continental Philosophy*, Oxford: OUP, 2001, pp. 119–20). However, as he goes on to note, 'obscurantism might not be a single thing' (p. 120), and there is also the case of 'obscure scientism' (p. 121). I follow this dissolving of his point further in the next but one footnote.
12. Stella Sandford, 'Johnny Foreigner', p. 44.
13. There is no doubt that the kinds of differences among the writings that one takes to heart can encourage different kinds of threats of emptiness. As we have just noted (note 11 above), Simon Critchley suggests that a distinctive threat for so-called Continental philosophy is 'obscurantism' and a distinctive threat for analytic philosophy is 'scientism'. Given the problems that immediately arise with this distinction (also noted above), Critchley invites us to devote time to developing 'a detailed taxonomy of the scientism/obscurantism distinction' (Simon Critchley, *Very Short Introduction to Continental Philosopy*, p. 121). But in view of (what Critchley also acknowledges to be) the profound diversity of ways of *going on* in philosophy within contemporary philosophy in general (indeed within philosophy historically) I would be strongly disinclined to try to count the ways in which philosophers can and do *go wrong* in the sense of becoming somehow empty. As Austin noted any distinction that can give a philosopher 'two shiny new concepts with which to crack the

crib of Reality' always also provides 'two new skids under our feet' (J. L Austin, *How To Do Things With Words*, Oxford: OUP, 1976, p. 25). As we saw, Critchley finds himself skidding almost immediately when he recognises the possibility of obscure scientism. I do not see how a more detailed taxonomy will help his distinction stand up again for much purpose.

14. If Continental philosophers are defined (as I will propose at a certain stage in the discussion below) as those *Anglophone* philosophers who do not confine their philosophical reading, for the most part, to authors in the analytic tradition, I hope that the future will see a growth in the number of such Continental philosophers. However, I would not expect many among them to feel any special resistance to reading texts from analytic philosophy too. A feature of those whose work encompasses serious study of (among others) the usual suspects today (those who one might call for that reason Continental philosophers) is that their own reading interests are characteristically *eclectic* rather than *exclusive*.

15. David West, *An Introduction to Continental Philosophy*, Oxford: Polity, 1996, p. 2.

16. Simon Critchley, *Very Short Introduction to Continental Philosophy*, p. 48.

17. Simon Critchley, *Very Short Introduction to Continental Philosophy*, p. 125.

18. Simon Critchley, *Very Short Introduction to Continental Philosophy*, p. 126.

19. Stella Sandford, 'Johnny Foreigner', p. 43.

20. See Appendix for details.

21. Nicely illustrating the generality of my point about 'police' placing those who do not (want to) place themselves, it is worth noting that (in what might also pass as a passing complement) Sandford represents me as belonging to the philosophical fold of those who work 'in the thriving non-xenophobic analytic and post-analytic scene' (Stella Sandford, 'Johnny Foreigner', p. 43).

22. Hugh Silverman, *Inscriptions: Between Phenomenology and Structuralism*, London: Routledge, p. 1987, p. 1.

23. The Appendix will show how distributions have altered recently. Only five years ago the majority of university teachers in the UK with research interests in some one or more of the usual suspects worked in departments where there were three or more colleagues with 'Continental' interests alongside them (forty out of seventy-three). By 2003/4 the figures had almost exactly reversed and the majority were by then either the sole representative in their department or have one other colleague who has research interests in this area (forty-three out of seventy-six). Moreover, the line up of 'centres' has changed and, in number terms, is, in that year, represented by Essex, Staffordshire and (goodness me) Oxford. The presence of Oxford in this line up is also reflected in its very high rating in this area in Brian Leiter's recent 'Philosophical Gourmet' report (http://www. philosophicalgourmet.com/breakdown.htm#28).

24. Personal communication.

25. Christopher Norris, *Minding the Gap*, Amherst, MA: University of Massachusetts Press, 2000, p. 104.
26. Numbers here are drawn from the *International Directory of Philosophers*, eds Ramona Cormier et al. Bowling Green, KY: Philosophy Documentation Center, 2004. Further statistical data from this bi-annual publication is presented in the Appendix.
27. For example, Christopher Janaway, now Professor of Philosophy at Southampton University, would be a good example of someone whose work (focused as it is on Schopenhauer) would place him somewhere in or near the final category. However, it would be absurd to think that this thereby placed him at the greatest philosophical distance from most analytic philosophers.
28. Mary Warnock, *The Philosophy of Sartre*, London: Hutchinson, 1965, p. 12.
29. I am particularly grateful to John Cottingham, Paul Davies, Brad Hooker, Fiona Hughes, Hanjo Glock, Catherine Lowe, Stephen Mulhall, Chris Norris, Peter Osborne, Stella Sandford, Sean Sayers, John Shand, Alessandra Tanesini, Jennie Walmsley and James Williams for their comments on material in this book. I also want to express my sincere thanks to those who attended and contributed to a seminar series that this text is based on held in the European Institute at the LSE in Michaelmas 2004/5. I am also grateful to an anonymous reader for some very interesting suggestions for approaching the idea of Continental philosophy from an American perspective. Most of all, however, I am grateful to Simon Critchley.

Appendix: Continental Philosophy in Britain since 1986

Statistics

The *International Directory of Philosophers* for 1986–89 details **forty** philosophers *identifying themselves* as having a specialism in (or in some generally recognised area of) Continental philosophy. Of these:

8 – were the single representative in a department
10 – were in a department with two representatives
18 – were in a department with three representatives
4 – were in a department with four representatives.

There was one department with four representatives: Warwick.

There were six departments with three representatives: Essex, Kent, Sussex, Queen's Belfast, Aberdeen, Glasgow.

The *International Directory of Philosophers* for 2001/2 details **seventy-three** philosophers *identifying themselves* as having a specialism in (or in some generally recognised area of) Continental philosophy. Of these:

20 – were the single representative in a department
14 – were in a department with two representatives
6 – were in a department with three representatives
16 – were in a department with four representatives
17 – were in a department with five or more representatives.

There were three departments with five or more representatives: Essex (six), Staffordshire (six) and Warwick (five).

There were four departments with four representatives: Lancaster, Middlesex, Sussex, Cardiff.

There were two departments with three representatives: Oxford and Dundee.

(No details were provided for Manchester Metropolitan University or Greenwich.)

The *International Directory of Philosophers* for 2003/4 details **seventy-six** philosophers *identifying themselves* as having a specialism in (or in some generally recognised area of) Continental philosophy. Of these:

15 – are the single representative in a department
28 – are in a department with two representatives
 9 – are in a department with three representatives
 8 – are in a department with four representatives
16 – are in a department with five representatives or more.

There are three departments with five or more representatives: Essex (five), Staffordshire (six), Oxford (five).

There are two departments with four representatives: Middlesex, Warwick.

There are three departments with three representatives: UEA, Dundee, Cardiff.

(No details were provided for Greenwich and details for Manchester Metropolitan look inaccurate and unreliable.)

Commentary

These statistics are at best a very rough guide to recent employment trends. Here are six reasons why.

1. There are people who are included here who would strongly resist being regarded as working in or on or even near 'Continental philosophy' (or even working in or on the tamer sounding 'Modern European philosophy') although the method of inclusion I have used – self-identification with a title that relates to a group or movement dominated by thinkers typically included among the usual suspects – includes them. For example, I have counted 'German philosophy' as a specialism to be included, but Hanjo Glock (who includes this in his own entry) is himself a Continental philosopher only in the extremely attenuated sense that he is himself German. (He once ironically apologised to the audience at an international conference on Wittgenstein that, unlike most serious scholars in the area, he would be working with the original German text.)

2. There are a growing number of people who are not included here who I personally think do work in some area that would be included but who do not take a label which could identify them as doing so. For example, Gordon Finlayson, now at Sussex but entered in 2003/4 under his previous appointment at York, lists his

specialisms as political and moral philosophy. Finlayson studied French and German at the University of St Andrews, and then took an MA in Continental philosophy and did his PhD on Hegel's criticism of Kant at the University of Essex. His central interests in political and moral philosophy are in Kant, Hegel, German idealism, twentieth-century German philosophy, the Frankfurt School, Adorno, Horkheimer and Habermas. His 'Continental' credentials are in that respect utterly impeccable – but he does not identify himself with this title or any related title in the Directory or on his departmental website, and so is not included in the list. What we might call the progressive 'becoming invisible' of the so-called 'Continental' specialism is I think the most distinctive feature of the lists, and probably indicates that 'ender' tendencies are presently more powerful than 'bender' ones. Whether one regards that as a good thing depends on which tendency is, in you, in the ascendancy.

3. Not all institutions seem to have made returns and some seem to have made incomplete returns. This is clearly the case with Greenwich University and Manchester Metropolitan University – institutions whose coverage in areas that would be included in these lists is well established and whose faculty would have bumped up the overall numbers.

4. As the example of Finlayson's move to Sussex indicates the details can become very rapidly out of date. And with such a small population to start with small changes can make statistically significant differences.

5. I have only examined three Directories.

6. The earliest Directory included here is strikingly different from the two more recent ones and seems in some ways to belong to another time. While, as far as I can see, academics were then as now invited to identify a research specialism *very* few actually did. So the number of philosophers who would have counted as having (but did not identify themselves as having) a specialism in (or in some generally recognised area of) Continental philosophy is almost certainly higher than the figure for those years suggests. In the biggest institutional listing, the members of the Sub-Faculty of Philosophy at the University of Oxford, only thirteen out of the seventy-six philosophers listed identified any research specialism at all, and that seems often connected to their holding one of the established Chairs and Readerships, for example: Peter Strawson, Waynflete Professor of Metaphysical Philosophy 1968–87, lists

'Metaphysics'; Michael Dummett, Wykeham Professor of Logic 1979–92, lists 'Logic'; Colin McGinn, Wilde Reader in Mental Philosophy 1985–90, lists 'Philosophy of Mind'. In the days before the Research Assessment Exercise took its grip on academic research activity in Britain I think most academic philosophers regarded themselves simply as philosophers and teachers of philosophy. No doubt the fact that nearly all of them were distinctively *analytic* philosophers helped that perception, just as it helped forge the emergence of a Continental residue.

These points taken, I would still want to suggest that some general trends can be spotted and some general conclusions drawn:

1. There are more people whose research lies in (or in some generally recognised area of) Continental philosophy than there used to be.
2. In recent years the growth is particularly strong outside the previously established 'centres' in this area. Indeed, there is some evidence that some of these centres are themselves moving away from their so-called Continental specialism.
3. In 2001/2 *most* people who worked in (or in some generally recognised area of) Continental philosophy were in departments with a strong profile in this area. In 2003/4 *most* people who worked in (or in some generally recognised area of) Continental philosophy were in departments where they are either alone or had one other colleague working in (or in some generally recognised area of) Continental philosophy. In addition, as I have noted, many people with serious working interests in one or other or some of the usual suspects do not list an identifiably 'Continental' specialism at all.
4. We do not need to suppose that those people who are alone or have only one other colleague working in (or in some generally recognised area of) Continental philosophy are especially isolated in their departments. They might be, but my experience and that of others I have spoken to is that a Continental-type specialism – self-identified or not – does not preclude good, sometimes excellent, working relationships with other colleagues in a department. One of the reasons for this is that few of those who have a research specialism in that area work or read *exclusively* in that area, and fewer analytic philosophers than hitherto are so hopelessly ignorant of and utterly hostile to work from that area.

General Conclusion

It would appear that a growing number of departments in Britain want to be able to provide their students with some experience of what has been called Continental philosophy, and are recruiting people with a research interest or specialism in this area or in some generally recognised sub-area thereof. This is what one might call the *normalisation* of Continental philosophy as a specialism in British philosophy.

With the normalisation of Continental philosophy in Britain, academics with research interests in this area will not only be found in special 'centres' but will increasingly be scattered across the country. And in so far as they are largely dominated by their 'ender' response they will be increasingly hard to spot too: they might well regard themselves as having research interests in political philosophy

- **Lucy Allais, Lecturer** – specialism: Kant's transcendental idealism.
- **Andrew Chitty, Lecturer** – specialism: Hegel, Marx, political philosophy, international political philosophy.
- **Charles Conti, Lecturer** – specialism: interdisciplinary links between literature, philosophy and theology.
- **Paul Davies, Reader** – specialism: Kantian and post-Kantian European philosophy, phenomenology, aesthetics, philosophy of literature, philosophy of religion.
- **Gordon Finlayson, Lecturer** – specialism: social and political philosophy, social theory, ethics ancient and modern, the history of philosophy.
- **Michael Morris, Reader** – specialism: philosophy of language, metaphysics, aesthetics, Wittgenstein, Plato.
- **Murali Ramachandran, Reader** – specialism: philosophical logic, philosophy of language, metaphysics, epistemology.
- **David Smith, Professor** – specialism: history of philosophy, phenomenology, metaphysics, philosophy of language, philosophy of mind and action, perception, philosophy of religion.
- **Tanja Staehler, Lecturer** – specialism: contemporary European philosophy (esp. Husserl, Heidegger, Merleau-Ponty, Levinas), German idealism, ancient philosophy (esp. Plato), Continental aesthetics.
- **Kathleen Stock, Lecturer** – specialism: imagination, moral imagination, imagination and the will.

Figure A.1 *Faculty of the Philosophy Department at the University of Sussex 2004/5.*

or philosophy of mind or philosophy of psychology or aesthetics or whatever.

I would suggest in closing that there is also the strong possibility that a new configuration is emerging: departments that are not readily identifiable as either analytic or Continental, departments which cannot be happily captured by those labels and which, for the most part, do without them themselves. This new configuration does not reflect that such departments have an 'equal share' of analytic and Continental philosophers but because the majority of faculty are not best understood in those terms at all. There is one department that already seems to me to have this new shape: the Department of Philosophy at Sussex University. In the Directory for 2003/4 I counted two philosophers who identified themselves as having a specialism in (or in some generally recognised area of) Continental philosophy. If I counted the department today I would get four (see Figure A.1 for Chitty, Davies, Smith and Staehler), but I think that would be an especially misleading report. The profile of the department is distinctive, original and interesting.[1]

Note

1. By way of illustration of the point that there are now some departments which cannot be happily captured by the analytic and Continental labels *and which do without them themselves*, it is worth noting that in the academic year 1999/2000 the Philosophy 'Subject Group' (as it was then called) at Sussex University replaced its old MA programme in 'Analytic and Continental philosophy' with a format that allows students to create their own pathways through courses focused around faculty research interests. Full-time students now take the core course 'Philosophical Topics' (a team taught course that aims to provide an advanced introduction to a number of central topics such as realism and idealism, the nature of perception, the possibility of knowledge, the nature of thought, freedom and determinism, the possibility of metaphysics, language and thought, moral truth) and one of the two courses 'Mind and Reality' (focusing on topics such as perception, knowledge, primary and secondary qualities, causation, realism and idealism) and 'Phenomenology' (exploring how different phenomenologists conceive of such issues as phenomenological method, the question of 'the other', and issues of language, art and history) in the Autumn Term. Students then take two courses out of a range of options in the Spring Term (options include courses on 'Language and Truth', 'Texts in the History of Philosophy', 'Political and Legal Philosophy', and a special paper connected to current faculty research interests). During the Summer Term students work under individual supervision towards a dissertation. While affirming in their

literature that this programme 'offers courses in analytical philosophy, Continental philosophy and the history of philosophy' the 'mixture' of faculty interests this is taken to reflect is not conceived as dividing individual members into different camps; on the contrary, the 'mixture' of interests occurs *within* and not only *between* faculty members.

Bibliography

Austin, J. L., *How To Do Things With Words*, Oxford: Oxford University Press, 1976.

Austin, J. L., 'A Plea for Excuses', in *Philosophical Papers*, Oxford: Clarendon, 1979.

Ash, Timothy Garton, *Free World*, London: Allen Lane, 2004.

Ayer, A. J. et al., *The Revolution in Philosophy*, London: Macmillan, 1957.

Baggini, Julian and Strangroom, Jeremy (eds), *New British Philosophy: The Interviews*, London: Routledge, 2002.

Bennington, Geoffrey, 'For the Sake of Argument', in *Arguing with Derrida*, ed. S. Glendinning, Oxford: Blackwell, 2001.

Carnap, Rudolph, 'Intellectual Autobiography', in P. A. Schlipp, *The Philosophy of Rudolph Carnap*, La Salle, IL: Open Court, 1963.

Cavell, Stanley, *The Claim of Reason*, Oxford: Oxford University Press, 1979.

Critchley, Simon, 'Introduction', in *A Companion to Continental Philosophy*, eds S. Critchley and W. Schroeder, Oxford: Blackwell, 1998.

Critchley, Simon, *Very Short Introduction to Continental Philosophy*, Oxford: Oxford University Press, 2001.

Cohen, L. J., *The Dialogue of Reason: An Analysis of Analytic Philosophy*, Oxford: Clarendon Press, 1986.

Cooper, David, 'Modern European Philosophy', in *The Blackwell Companion to Philosophy*, eds N. Bunnin and E. P. Tsui-James, Oxford: Blackwell, 1996.

Cormier, Ramona et al., *International Directory of Philosophers*, Bowling Green, KY: Philosophy Documentation Center, 1986–2004.

Denoon Cumming, Robert, *Human Nature and History*, 2 vols, Chicago: Chicago University Press, 1969.

Denoon Cumming, Robert, *Phenomenology and Deconstruction*, 4 vols, Chicago: Chicago University Press, 1991–2001.

Denoon Cumming, Robert, 'Role-Playing: Sartre's Transformation of Husserl's Phenomenology', in *Cambridge Companion to Sartre*, ed. C. Howells, Cambridge: Cambridge University Press, 1992.

Denyer, Nicholas, 'The Charms of Jacques Derrida', *Cambridge Review*, vol. 113, no. 2318, 1992, pp. 103–5.

Derrida, Jacques, 'Structure Sign and Play in the Human Sciences', in *Writing and Difference*, London: Routledge, 1978.

Derrida, Jacques, *The Post Card*, Chicago: University of Chicago Press, 1987.

Derrida, Jacques, *Limited Inc*, Evanston, IL: Northwestern University Press, 1988.

Derrida, Jacques, in *Arguing with Derrida*, ed. S. Glendinning, Oxford: Blackwell, 2001.

Derrida, Jacques, *Who's Afraid of Philosophy*, Stanford, CA: Stanford University Press, 2002.

Diamond, Cora, 'Throwing Away the Ladder', in *The Realistic Spirit*, Cambridge, MA: MIT Press, 1991.

Dummett, Michael, interview with Fabrice Pataut, *Philosophical Investigations*, vol. 19, no. 1, 1996, pp. 1–33.

Friedman, Michael, *A Parting of the Ways*, Chicago: Open Court, 2000.

Glendinning, Simon (ed.), *The Edinburgh Encyclopedia of Continental Philosophy*, Edinburgh: Edinburgh University Press, 1999.

Glendinning, Simon, 'Introduction', *The Encyclopedia of Continental Philosophy*, ed. S. Glendinning, Edinburgh: Edinburgh University, 1999.

Glendinning, Simon (ed.), *Arguing with Derrida*, Oxford: Blackwell, 2001.

Glendinning, Simon, *New British Philosophy: The Interviews*, eds J. Baggini and J. Strangroom, London: Routledge, 2002.

Glendinning, Simon, 'Language', in *Understanding Derrida*, eds J. Reynolds and J. Roffe, London: Continuum, 2004.

Glendinning, Simon, 'What is Phenomenology?', *Think*, no. 7, 2004, pp. 33–41.

Glock, H.-J., ' "Clarity" is not Enough', in *Wittgenstein and the Future of Philosophy: Proceedings of the 24th International Wittgenstein Symposium*, eds R. Haller and K. Puhl, Vienna: Hölder-Pichler-Tempsky, 2002.

Glock, H.-J., 'Was Wittgenstein an Analytic Philosopher?', *Metaphilosophy*, vol. 35, no. 4, 2004, pp. 419–44.

Hare, R. M., 'A School for Philosophers', *Ratio*, vol. 2, no. 2, 1960, pp. 107–20.

Heidegger, Martin, *Being and Time*, Oxford: Blackwell, 1962.

Hume, David, *Enquiries Concerning Human Understanding*, Oxford: Oxford University Press, 1975.

Keat, Russell et al., *Understanding Phenomenology*, Oxford: Blackwell, 1980.

Levinas, Emmanuel, *Totality and Infinity*, Pittsburgh: Duquesne University Press, 1969.

Locke, John, *An Essay Concerning Human Understanding*, ed. A. D. Woozley, Glasgow: Collins, 1964.

McCumber, John, *Time in the Ditch*, Evanston, IL: Northwestern University Press 2001.

Merleau-Ponty, Maurice, *Texts and Dialogues with Merleau-Ponty*, eds H. Silverman and J. Barry, New York: Humanities Press, 1992.

Monk, Ray, 'Bertrand Russell's Brainchild', *Radical Philosophy*, 78, 1996, pp. 2–5.

Moran, Dermot, *Introduction to Phenomenology*, London: Routledge, 2000.

Mulhall, Stephen, *Inheritance and Originality*, Oxford: Oxford University Press, 2001.

Norris, Christopher, *Derrida*, London: Fontana Press, 1987.

Norris, Christopher, *Minding the Gap*, Amherst, MA: University of Massachusetts Press, 2000.

Passmore, John, *A Hundred Years of Philosophy*, London: Penguin, 1957.

Pippin, Robert, *Modernism as a Philosophical Problem*, 2nd edn, Oxford: Blackwell 1999.

Putnam, Hilary, 'Levinas and Judaism', in *The Cambridge Companion to Levinas*, eds S. Critchley and R. Bernasconi, Cambridge: Cambridge University Press, 2002.

Quine, W. V. O., 'Two Dogmas of Empiricism', in *From a Logical Point of View*, New York: Harper, 1963.

Rée, Jonathan, 'English Philosophy in the Fifties', *Radical Philosophy*, 65, 1993, pp. 3–21.

Rhees, Rush (ed.), *Recollections of Wittgenstein*, Oxford: Oxford University Press, 1984.

Rorty, Richard, *Contingency, Irony and Solidarity*, Cambridge: Cambridge University Press, 1989.

Rorty, Richard, 'Introduction', to W. Sellars, *Empiricism and the Philosophy of Mind*, Cambridge, MA: Harvard University Press, 1997.

Ryle, Gilbert, 'Phenomenology versus *The Concept of Mind*', in *Collected Papers*, London: Hutchinson, 1971.

Ryle, Gilbert, 'Phenomenology', in *Collected Papers*, London: Hutchinson, 1971.

Sallis, John, *Delimitations*, Bloomington, IN: Indiana University Press, 1995.

Sandford, Stella, 'Johnny Foreigner', *Radical Philosophy*, no. 102, 2000, pp. 42–5.

Searle, John, 'Contemporary Philosophy in the United States', in *The Blackwell Companion to Philosophy*, eds N. Bunnin and E. P. Tsui-James, Oxford: Blackwell 1996.

Silverman, Hugh, *Inscriptions: Between Phenomenology and Structuralism*, London: Routledge, 1987.

Silverman, Hugh, *Philosophy and Non-Philosophy since Merleau-Ponty*, ed. H. J. Silverman, London: Routledge, 1988.

Warnock, Geoffrey, *English Philosophy Since 1900*, Oxford: Oxford University Press, 1958.

Warnock, Geoffrey, '*Mind* under Gilbert Ryle's Editorship', *Mind*, LXXXV, 1976, pp. 47–56.

Warnock, Mary, *The Philosophy of Sartre*, London: Hutchinson, 1965.

West, David, *An Introduction to Continental Philosophy*, Oxford: Polity, 1996.

Wheeler III, Samuel, *Deconstruction as Analytic Philosophy*, Stanford, CT: Stanford University Press, 2000.

Williams, Bernard, 'Contemporary Philosophy: A Second Look', in *The Blackwell Companion to Philosophy*, eds N. Bunnin and E. P. Tsui-James, Oxford: Blackwell, 1996.

Williamson, Timothy, *New British Philosophy: The Interviews*, eds J. Baggini and J. Strangroom, London: Routledge, 2002.

Wittgenstein, Ludwig, *Philosophical Investigations*, Oxford: Blackwell, 1958.

Index

Adorno, Theodor, 51, 55, 63
Allan, Raymond B., 98, 99
Althusser, Louis, 54, 61, 63
America, analytic philosophy in
  'Continentals' as 'enemy within',
    99–100, 101
  McCarthyism, 98–101
  philosophical origins of, 99
analytic/Continental distinction
  as belonging to what is rotten in
    contemporary philosophy, 4–5,
    21, 69
  as contentious/perverse (West),
    94–5
  de facto distinction, 94, 115,
    119–20
  as deep opposition, 5, 7–8
  philosophical culture, division
    within, 103–5, 109
  power and cultural reach of, 9–10
  as problematic, 2–4
  'problems' *versus* 'proper names',
    40–1
  reasons for maintaining, 115, 117
  as reception-response, 10–11,
    122, 123
  scientism *versus* obscurantism,
    125–6n13, 125n11
  'so-called' distinction, Derrida on,
    8–9
  and willingness not to read well, 6
  see also gulf-seeking
analytic philosophy
  'at a glance' (Glock), 14f, 35
  British origins of, 99, 100
  difference, insistence on, 22
  empiricist to post-Kantian phase,
    81–2

  institutional dominance of, 120–2
  naturalistic wing in, 90n62
  as revolutionary movement, 79,
    80, 87n46, 101, 111–12n51
  see also America, analytic
    philosophy in
Anglophone Continental
  philosophers
  appropriation of title, 13, 15, 84
  research interest distributions *see*
    university departments,
    representation of Continental
    philosophy in
  see also Continental philosophy,
    degree programmes in
Arendt, Hannah, 51, 61
Austin, J. L., 23, 25, 26, 27, 31, 34,
  87n46, 99, 111–12n51

Badiou, Alain, 56, 64
Barthes, Roland, 53, 62, 63
Baudrillard, Jean, 54
Bauer, Bruno, 60
Bauer, Edgar, 60
Beauvoir, Simone de, 52, 60, 61
Being, question of (Heidegger), 49,
  75–7
Being and Nothingness (Sartre),
  124–5
Benjamin, Walter, 49–50, 63
Bennington, Geoffrey, 118
Bergson, Henri, 46, 59
Bloch, Ernst, 48–9, 63
Bloom, Harold, 100–1
Bosanquet, Bernard, 80, 89
Bradley, F. H., 80, 88
Breda, Herman van, 71
Brentano, Franz, 45, 47, 60, 61

Index

Varela, Francisco, 36n6

Warnock, Geoffrey, 79–82, 84, 88
Warnock, Mary, 124–5
Weber, Max, 48, 61
Weil, Felix, 63
West, David, 94–5, 96, 97
Wheeler, Samuel, 31
Whitehead, A. N., 89

Williams, Bernard, 32, 85n11
Williamson, Timothy, 32
Wittgenstein, Ludwig, 14f, 23, 26,
 27, 31, 34, 72, 73, 81, 84

Young Hegelians, 59–60

Žižek, Slavoj, 57, 64